BEWARE
THE DEVIL

BEWARE THE DEVIL

ROBERT LEE
with
David Lee

Marshall Pickering

Marshall Morgan & Scott
Marshall Pickering
3 Beggarwood Lane, Basingstoke, Hants., UK.

First published by Marshall Morgan & Scott 1983
Part of the Marshall Pickering Holdings Group
A subsidiary of the Zondervan Corporation

All Biblical quotations taken from the
Revised Standard Version.

Reissued with a new cover 1988

ISBN 0 551 01063 0

Printed in Great Britain by
Hazell Watson & Viney Limited, Aylesbury, Bucks

Contents

Preface

Many of the events recorded in this book happened over twenty years ago. There are obvious technical difficulties in reconstructing a story after so long a time interval. Conversations, in particular, become blurred in the memory and cannot be set down here in their original form. I hope that, where additions have been made, they help the reader to understand the background to the story, and do not distort the truth. Most names and places have been changed to protect the people involved.

Robert Lee

1. The slave

When I awoke on Tuesday, 11th April, 1961, I knew I couldn't carry on any longer.

I groped for the alarm clock. The first thing my fingers touched in the darkness was a small, screw-topped bottle. Sleeping pills. I had taken three the previous night. Fearing that I might knock it over I laid the bottle on its side before continuing my search. Eventually I found the clock and held its luminous face in front of me. The time was five-thirty. I had slept for precisely one hour.

Sighing, I passed a hand through my hair and sank back on to the pillow. I had no idea how I was going to survive the day, and certainly no inclination to get up and begin it. Instead I lay staring into the gloomy recesses of the room. A nearby street-lamp glowed dimly through the curtains, throwing into silhouette the great oval mirror of the dressing table. Opposite, and hidden in a well of shadow, stood the tall, mahogany wardrobe passed down to me by my parents. In the space between I could just make out the twin bed in which my wife, Joanna, lay sleeping. Everything looked so normal. But, of course, it wasn't. Nothing in my life was normal any more.

'You're wasting time,' said a voice.

Nothing had moved. Nobody else was in the room.

I groaned. 'Leave me alone.'

'The training must start at once.'

'Look, can't you see I'm nearly dead from exhaustion? You can't expect me to work for you if you don't give me any rest.'

The voice made a sound as if its owner was clicking his tongue. 'God's not going to like that. He doesn't like the training to be delayed.'

'I don't care about the training,' I hissed, trying to keep my voice down. 'It's not doing me any good. As far as I'm concerned God can forget the training and leave me alone.'

'You mean you don't want to have miraculous powers of healing?' The voice had assumed a tone of calculated astonishment.

I hesitated. 'Yes. Yes, of course I do. But what guarantee do I have that you're ever going to give them to me?'

'You have to trust us.'

'Trust you!' I responded angrily. 'You don't deserve to be trusted. Nothing you tell me to do ever works out right. At the office last week you told me Phyllis's mother had died, and when I asked her she didn't know what I was talking about. People are starting to think I'm crazy. My own family thinks I'm crazy. A whole year now I've trusted you, and where has it got me? Nowhere. I just get more suffering.'

I broke off. I could hear Joanna stirring. She called out, 'Robert', and then there was silence. Perhaps she was talking in her sleep.

I went on, in a suppressed whisper, 'Look, please, I've had enough. I know I said I would do whatever you wanted, but there's a limit. I can't take any more. Tell God I'm sorry. I'm contracting out.'

'You can't.'

The blunt refusal pricked me. I had known men at work who'd tried it on like that, and I knew how to handle them. 'Then I'll get rid of you,' I said in a sudden flash of anger.

I didn't mean it. I'd long since learned that there was no point in resistance.

'Will you?' said the voice. It showed no anxiety, only a faintly mocking surprise. I cursed myself for speaking out, and awaited the reprisal. It wasn't long in coming. Suddenly a stabbing pain shot through my back and pinned me to the bed by an incredibly powerful force.

'Will you?' repeated the voice.

I struggled feebly. This experience of being physically attacked wasn't new. It had happened on and off over the last few months, more so recently. But the pain had never been so severe, or the force that held me down so irresistible. I felt beads of perspiration running down over my temples. I was starting to choke.

'No, no, no,' I gasped. 'I won't get rid of you!'

Immediately the pain eased. I lay gulping the air.

'Good,' said the voice. 'You wouldn't want God to be angry with you, would you?'

I could only shake my head. The voice, which was sometimes caressing, sometimes stern, but always unperturbed, went on in a matter-of-fact way, 'You need me, Robert. Don't forget that. I am your Guide. I was lucky I found you when you were looking for God, or you might have got lost. God's going to do great things with you, Robert. You're an important man. You're a big part of God's plan. When you've been fully trained all sorts of people are going to look up to you. You remember Joe Wilson, that little rat who used to keep his thumb on you? He'll look up to you too. He'll be licking your boots. There'll be nothing you can't have when that time comes. But you must be trained first of all. God's got to work on you.'

The words washed over me like warm, gentle waves. The voice knew how to get its way. The stick and the carrot were plied in alternation until the ass moved. I whimpered, 'But the training, I'm so tired of it all. Can't it stop, soon?'

It was a hopeless request. There was no reason to suppose I had completed the programme of work set for me, or was anywhere near completing it. The only encouragement I got from this Guide – or the other voices he consorted with – was an occasional comment that God was 'pleased'. No concrete commitments were made. I was never told that the training would finish in a stated length of time. When I asked I was invariably told it would be over 'soon'. And 'soon' could stretch a long way, especially if I did something to annoy them, like asking how much more there was to come.

I listened to the voices consulting in whispers I could not understand. At length the Guide came forward.

'We've asked God,' he said, 'and he says your training should stop today.'

I could hardly believe my ears. I half sat up in bed. 'Today? You mean it's nearly finished?'

'That's what God says.'

'Then am I going to be a healer?'

'God keeps his promises. You have served him faithfully, and he is going to reward you. This afternoon you will have your first introduction to the healing powers: you will receive the name of God.' There was a pause, then he added, 'There is just one more task to do for your training.'

'Of course,' I said brightly. 'What do you want me to do?'

'You will deliver a message.'

'Saying what?'

'We'll tell you that when you get there. Just go to 12 Belacre Drive on your way to work.'

A slight doubt drifted across my mind, and I frowned. I had been on other errands of this sort. But before I had time even to censure the thought the voice had responded, 'Careful. God won't approve of that. The schedule can be delayed, you know . . .'

'I'm sorry.'

But in the training being sorry was never quite good enough. The pain in my spine intensified. It was like an electric shock.

'I'm sorry. I said I'm sorry!'

I expected another reprimand, but none came. All I could hear was a mutter of conversation, fairly loud but indistinct. For the meantime at least the Guide seemed to have gone away. I threw back the covers and swung my legs out of bed. My head ached badly; had it been possible I would have laid back down and slept the whole day through. But there was a job to do, and of course the Guide wouldn't leave me alone for long.

Wearily, I got up and made for the bathroom. As I reached the door Joanna called out quietly, 'Robert, are you all right?'

'Yes. I'm all right,' I replied, a note of irritation in my voice. What could I say? Several times I had tried to explain what was happening to me, how seances and the ouija board had led me into the world of the spirits and enslaved me to its masters. But although she was a spiritist, and came from a family of spiritists, Joanna had never been spoken to by a spiritual being; to her, spiritism was a source of comfort, a means of contact with dead loved ones on the 'other side'. It was totally harmless.

I wished I could show her the Guide, just so that she would know my suffering was real. But not even I had seen him. He had a personality and a voice, but no body. And the only person who could hear him was me. Joanna was conscious only of the furtive, one-sided conversations during the night, and my increasingly irrational behaviour. All I could do was try and cover up as best

I could and pretend everything was normal. I wasn't doing very well.

The light in the bathroom made me blink. I fumbled in the cupboard for my electric razor, plugged it in and leaned towards the mirror. It was my habit to shave in the morning before I did anything else; I didn't feel clean until I'd shaved. This morning, however, I paused at seeing my reflection in the glass.

I looked sick. There were dark shadows under my eyes. My hair, combed back off a tall forehead, was greasy and streaked with grey. I turned my head first one way then the other, pressing my fingers down the cheeks, and finally stood back and gazed at myself for several seconds. The height was still there, and the broad shoulders. But the alertness and the executive composure were fading fast. I'm only forty-six,' I thought. 'But I look like I'm pushing sixty.'

I bent forward again and switched on the shaver. It was an old model and in the confined space of the bathroom set up an abrasive buzzing. I had meant to replace it, but in a way I was glad I hadn't because it drowned out the voices. I pondered on what the Guide had said. Perhaps, after all, this was to be the last day of suffering. Hadn't he said so? Surely after all the misery he'd put me through I deserved it. For months now I hadn't slept more than three hours in a night. Usually much less. There was always some kind of work to be done on me. God says this, God says that. It was inevitably unpleasant and often extremely painful. Still, it was worth it if in the end I was going to be a healer for God himself. And the Guide had often hinted that considerable financial rewards might come as well.

A small flush of excitement came over me, the same sort that had come when I was promoted to my present senior executive position. That job was the culmination of twenty years' hard slog in the electricity business. It was inconceivable to me that promotion should not also occur in the world of spirits. Even so a doubt entered my mind. The Guide had told me lies before — why should he not be lying again? But it was God, not the Guide, who had said that the training would stop, and I refused to believe that God would lie. The being who created the universe must be incapable of an outright lie, almost by definition.

Feeling a bit more cheerful I put the shaver away, washed my face in cold water and, pulling on the dressing-gown I'd left in the bathroom the previous night, went downstairs. The kitchen was cold. I put on the kettle then turned to the window. The radiator was just beginning to get warm. I leaned against it, elbows on the sill, my breath making a circle of condensation on the glass.

Outside dawn was breaking. The garden, well kept with paths and flower beds running down each side, terminated in a wire fence and a row of cherry trees. One of them was in full blossom; the ground beneath it was strewn with fallen blooms, like pink confetti. Through the gap between the trees I could just see the church on Loughton Hill, with its green, copper spire.

We had moved here, Joanna, the children and I, in the November of 1959. Socially, Loughton was quite an achievement. *Pendragon*, which had been built entirely to specification, was so far the only house on a new cul-de-sac. It symbolised a decisive step in my struggle for success. I had, I felt, received a bad start in life owing to my father's mismanagement of my schooling. To his death I never quite forgave him for it. Both schools had seemed to inhibit my education, with the result that by the age of sixteen I was fit only to collect money from electricity meters in Hackney. For that I earned twenty-five shillings a week. The shame of it was intolerable. I rebelled and signed on for the HND course at Regent Street Polytechnic, determined to remedy the situation. It took me eight years to become a chartered electrical engineer, and another twenty to claw my way up in the electricity supply industry.

Now I had, in a palpable sense, made it. But as I gazed out on that peaceful suburban scene I gathered not a shred of enjoyment. My achievements, my home, my wife, my children − all that had once meant so much to me − now appeared drab and remote. Every ounce of pleasure had been leached away by the voices and their ceaseless training. I could hear them right now, whispering and conferring somewhere in the dress circle of my mind. Soon one of them, probably the Guide, would turn his attention to me again for the next round of instructions and taunts. I closed my eyes. 'No,' I thought. 'I'm doing this for God. Soon all this suffering will end and I will be free again. He won't let it go on for ever.'

'Robert, the kettle's boiling!'

I turned to see Joanna striding across the kitchen. I had quite

14

forgotten about the kettle. A great cloud of steam was pouring up towards the ceiling. I stood there stupidly while she switched it off.

'Honestly, Robert. What's the matter with you?'

I shrugged. 'My mind had wandered. Sorry.'

We both knew I was hedging. She glared at me for a moment, then turned aside and began the morning ritual of coffee and toast as if I were no longer in the room. She was still a very good-looking woman; the fleck of white in her hair would lend an air of refinement to her middle age. My love for her was as strong as it had ever been. I watched her morosely, nursing inside me an unspoken grudge against the Guide for driving us apart. When she stirred the coffee the clink of the spoon seemed unusually loud in the silence between us.

'Lovely day,' I said, trying to make conversation. 'I thought I might do some gardening after work tonight.'

She handed me the cup without replying and sat down at the table. Silence fell again. I stood blowing on my drink, feeling stiff and uncomfortable. At length Joanna said, 'What are you going to do about it?'

'About what?'

She let out a small, exasperated cluck. 'For heaven's sake, Robert, you're on the verge of a breakdown.'

'I'm all right.'

'You know perfectly well you're not.'

'I'm all right, I tell you.'

'Do you mean to tell me that talking to yourself for half the night is *normal?*'

'I'm not sleeping, that's all.'

'Well, neither am I.'

'Joanna!' I paused, trying to keep myself calm. 'Look, I know I've been under a lot of strain. I told you about the voices and the pictures. They've been worse than usual lately. But today it's all going to change.'

'How do you know?'

I hesitated. Somehow I couldn't bring myself to say, 'They said so'.

Joanna sat with her arms folded on the table, looking straight ahead of her. 'I wish you'd go and see a medium,' she said.

'I've been to scores of mediums already.'

'One of them must be able to help you.'

'Darling, no medium can help me. It's hopeless. You remember that first chap I saw – Quentin whatever-he's-called? He's supposed to be one of the top dogs, and all he did was go into a trance and drivel. I couldn't get a sensible remark out of him for the whole hour I was there.'

I had been very dissatisfied with that visit, and would have said more, but I felt the voices stirring inside me. I was being disloyal.

'None of this would have happened if you hadn't been so enthusiastic,' Joanna said.

'That's right. Blame it on me.'

'It's true. You threw yourself into spiritism just like you threw yourself into your job and your home movies. You won't do anything by halves. You drive yourself until you're nearly exhausted over it, and never spare a thought for anyone else. We're the ones that suffer, the children and I. It's murder having to live with you when you're in a state like this. When are you going to learn to do things in moderation?'

In a way she was right. It was I who had come up with the grand idea of investigating the occult; it was I who had followed the trail to its bitter end, attending seances and making the family play ouija with me. No one had egged me on. And summary justice had been dealt out in the fact that it was I and not they who now suffered the consequences. They couldn't understand my predicament. I had cut myself adrift.

'Well, what am I supposed to do about it?' I demanded, angry and helpless.

'Just co-operate.'

'Why should I?'

'Robert, you're so headstrong!'

'OK, OK. What are you suggesting?'

'Go and see someone.'

She paused. I had thrown my hands up in despair.

'There you go again. Robert, listen to me. I was talking to Mummy, and she knows a man who's very experienced in this sort of thing. He's willing to give you a consultation. You only have to phone him.'

'Another medium, I take it?'

'Yes, but – '

I waved her explanations aside. 'I'm sorry, the answer is no. I've consulted too many mediums already. None of them can help. I've phoned them in the dead of night and been told to take a strong coffee and go back to bed. I'm finished with mediums. They may be able to call up the spirits of the dead, but they've never helped me. Besides, the past is past. I'm out of the wood now. You can tell your mother thank-you-very-much, but I don't need any more mediums.'

With an air of finality I took my cup and raised it to my lips. It was intended to be a casual, confident motion. But as my fingers closed round the handle, an alien force entered my hand and jerked the cup upwards. I cried out as the hot liquid splashed into my face, and dropped the cup on the floor. It shivered into pieces. I stood dumbfounded, coffee dripping off my chin and dressing-gown. In the distance I heard a peal of mocking laughter.

Joanna had jumped to her feet. She drew in a breath, and for a second we were motionless, facing each other across the kitchen. Then she turned on her heel and left the room. The door slammed behind her.

I could feel my heart thudding in my chest. At my feet the blue floor tiles were smeared with coffee and broken china. I bent down and started collecting the pieces, dimly aware of Joanna's voice in the hall, speaking to the children and directing them away from the kitchen. I hated being explained. One phrase that I caught was 'Daddy's being silly again'. It mortified me. I loved my children dearly, and what did they hear about their father? That he was being silly again. Again! It had become a constant condition.

Five minutes later I had more or less cleared up the mess. No one came in, so I cooked myself some porridge and sat eating it moodily at the table. After that it was time to get dressed. By eight o'clock when I was ready to leave. I had not spoken another word to anyone in the house. The eldest children, Jill and Bob, stayed out of my way, and Joanna, though I passed her more than once on the landing, looked firmly in the other direction. Only David, who was too young to know what was going on, tottered up to the front door to wave goodbye.

I had left the car, a new maroon Consul, out on the drive. It was an elegant vehicle, another one of my 'achievements'. I tossed my briefcase on to the passenger seat and clambered in. But before putting the key in the ignition I leaned forward to rest my head on the wheel. The sleepless night was beginning to tell. I could keep on going for a couple of hours, but after that a terrible urge came over me to close my eyes, to put aside whatever I was doing and collapse into sleep. Many times the only thing that had stopped me was the perpetual banter of conversation going on in my mind. It stopped me now. The familiar voice came forward and said, 'Belacre Drive'.

I drove out on to the High Road and cruised towards the station. The small hump of a bridge led down past the shopping parade then up in the direction of St Anselm's Church. I knew Belacre Drive was one of the side streets on the estate east of the church. I took a right turn and drove around until I found it. Number twelve was near the top. I parked the car outside the house but did not get out. I was awaiting instructions.

'Well, I'm here. What now?'

'Go to the door,' the Guide answered.

I got out of the car. The house, a large detached one with a white stucco finish and window shutters, bore the name *Gossander*. I'd never seen it before in my life. I walked up to the studded oak door and after a moment's hesitation pounded on the knocker. The next few seconds were virtual torture. I found myself hoping fervently that whoever occupied the house was on holiday, or in the bath. But no, there were footsteps approaching. 'What do I say?' I hissed.

The door opened on a tall, elderly man in a cardigan and carpet slippers. He had a pipe in his mouth, but he did not remove it He just raised his eyebrows in a gesture of inquiry.

In my mind I threw out one last desperate plea for assistance. None came. Suddenly I panicked. I opened my mouth in the wild hope that words would be placed inside it. They weren't – what emerged was a low moan of the sort our dog made when it was sick. This needed to be disguised, so I turned it into a cough. But the cough gave me such a tickle in the throat that pretty soon I was doubled up in a fit of coughing.

All this the man watched with a good-humoured frown. When I had recovered a little he said simply, 'Can I get you a glass of water?'

I shook my head.

18

'Then what else may I do for you?'

'I have a message,' I spluttered.

'Oh.' He gave a faint smile. 'From whom?'

I cast my mind around frantically. 'From God,' I said at last.

'You don't sound very sure.'

'No. Er, yes – '

'If you're from the Jehovah's Witnesses I think you might do better to try next door. They're church-goers.' He started to close the door.

'No, I'm not a Jehovah's Witness. I'm – ' I put a hand over my eyes. 'I'm sorry. I think I must have come to the wrong address.'

'I think you must. Not to worry.'

He smiled gently and put the pipe back in his mouth. I stumbled back down the path, burning with shame and indignation. 'Why?' I snarled as I clapped the car door closed and revved the engine, 'Why did you humiliate me?' The car lurched out into the road. 'Why send me to a house I don't know, to a man I've never laid eyes on, then give me nothing to say?'

'You did very well,' said the voice.

'Thank you very much!'

'You have proved your faith in God.'

'Oh, for heaven's sake! What possible use can it be to endure a farce like that?'

'It was a test of your faith. Remember, you have to trust us.'

There was a slight note of menace in this last remark. I checked myself. 'All right,' I said. 'Just keep your promise, that's all.'

'Of course. God is very pleased with you.'

I reached the office rather quicker than usual. A brief flash of sunshine made the windows glint brightly as I approached. To the right lay the old tram depot, only recently closed down and now serving as a warehouse. Some of the tram rails were still visible on the forecourt. They bumped slightly under the wheels as I turned off the main road, down a side street, and left into the office car park. It was a small, open yard with only two covered parking spaces. One of these belonged to the manager, the other to me. Both were empty. I nosed the Consul up to the white painted sign that bore my name, and stopped.

The drive had dispelled some of my frustration, but I was still pretty sore. The Guide's supercillious attitude irked me; my trials seemed to him a mere matter of routine. He was like a seasoned officer putting a young recruit through his paces. If I fell face down in the mud it would be no more to him than a good story to tell in the mess. Yet – I told myself repeatedly – it was for my own good. I had to hang on. I dared not give vent to the rebellious feelings that churned deep inside me. If I persevered, in a matter of hours I would be free.

I locked the car and set out over the tarmac, briefcase tucked under my arm. A few ragged, grey clouds were chasing each other across the sky. At the main entrance Fred, the doorman, nodded and smiled.

'Morning, Mr Lee.'

'Hello, Fred.'

'Looks like rain.'

'I hope not. I'm planning to dig the garden tonight.'

Fred shook his head and frowned. 'I'd say we were in for a downpour.'

'Well, I trust your judgment, Fred,' I replied, making for the lift.

Fred watched me go past. 'Day was, Mr Lee, when you'd have taken the stairs. Young man like you ought to be ashamed of himself, if you'll forgive me for saying so.'

'Overweight,' I said, pinching my stomach and pressing the lift button for the sixth storey. 'Blame it on the canteen staff.' But he was right. No so long ago I'd have taken the stairs at a run, just to prove I could do it. Today, when the lift came, I leaned heavily on the handrail all the way up.

At the top a strong smell of floor polish had lingered overnight. I stepped out, hoping I was the first to arrive and that I wouldn't have to talk to anyone before I reached my office. But I bumped into Phyllis – the person I least wanted to meet because since receiving my misdirected inquiry about her mother she had started to fuss over me. She immediately asked after my health, and I spent five miserable minutes trying to look cheerful until the manager appeared. The subject of conversation abruptly changed to golf. The working day was safely underway, and we dispersed to our respective offices.

My own, on a clear day, commanded a rather impressive view of the East London docklands. I often sat on the large centre table to look out over the city. This table had a glass top, under which lay an Ordnance Survey map, altered by the drawing office to show administrative areas. At its top end lay my desk, with a marble penholder and blotting pad, and behind that the leathered, revolving chair that I'd recently inherited from the manager.

I sat down and began sorting through the contents of my in-tray. The morning crawled by. When I had finished with the correspondence I called in the chief of administration, Stan Jordan, to talk over the technical development programme. All the time the voices muttered in my head. More than once I had to ask Stan to repeat himself because I'd been distracted from what he was saying. At last we finished and it was time for lunch.

Often I would go home during the lunch break, but I felt no inclination to do so today. I went in early to the canteen and took a secluded seat near a window. It looked as though Fred was right; cloud had now gathered across most of the sky. I chewed without enthusiasm, gazing out over the roofs of London. 'A few hours,' I told myself, 'a few hours, and it will be over.' I wondered when it would happen. 'This afternoon' was all that the Guide had said. I realised I was looking forward to my release with a mixture of longing and fear.

Leaving most of my food on the plate, I got up and walked back to the office. As usual at lunchtime there were a lot of people milling around in the corridors. Outside my office some of the clerical workers were talking and laughing; they recognised me at once and stepped aside. I entered, closing the door behind me.

Inside, it was strangely quiet. The conversation outside, which I would normally have been able to hear quite distinctly, seemed very far away. I glanced round the room. Everything was in place, exactly as I had left it. At the same time I got a curious sensation that it had been disturbed. I circled the large committee table and, with slow, deliberate movements, seated myself behind my desk.

The whole office now lay before me, silent and empty. For a few minutes I sat very still and watched it. Windows ran the whole length of the west wall, yet the room was abnormally dark, darker than it should have been at this time of day. I had a sense of being closed in. The flimsy partition that separated my own office from the next had taken on the appearance of stone. Beyond the windows no roofs and chimneys were visible, only a grey pall of cloud. Suddenly the outside world seemed as distant from me as if I were buried a thousand feet underground.

The promised time had arrived. I knew it.

When the shadows on the far wall began to shift and circulate it came almost as a relief. They rose like wisps of smoke, turning in an anticlockwise motion. I looked on. Slowly the shadows resolved themselves into a face — a mean, bestial face with heavy brows and eyes slitted like those of a cat — yet no sooner had the picture formed than it dissolved again. I wondered if I had really seen the face, or imagined it. The shadows kept on turning. Their motion had a soothing, almost hypnotic effect.

Then, on the fringes of my mind, I heard the voice of the Guide. 'Pick up the pen,' he said.

I looked down. There on my blotting pad was a clean sheet of paper. Beside it, in the holder, a fountain pen. I gazed at them numbly, unable to remember whether I had placed them there or not. The Guide's voice jolted me into action. I raised my hand slowly over the desk and grasped the pen. So far the motion was entirely under my own control, though it required an effort, as if I was pushing the pen through oil. I lifted the pen and it came to rest, hovering. Then the Guide's voice came again.

'Are you prepared?'

'Yes'.

'Relax your hand .. '

I obeyed; my arm should have slumped down on the blotter, but it stayed suspended.

'It is time for you to know the name of God. We shall write it together.'

Once again my hand moved — but this time I had no control over it. Physically, I was exerting all the pressure necessary to push my hand forward, but something else determined the actions it performed. I watched it descend on to the paper. It began to write; two letters, three, were completed in extravagant loops on the page, quite different from my own handwriting. As the minutes passed the writing got harder and harder, until my fingers ached. At last the pen reached the end of the page and stopped. There was a pause.

'You can rest now,' I heard the guide say. 'The name of God is a very long one. We'll write the other twenty-six letters to-morrow.' I heaved a sigh of relief and looked down at God's name: ZQROCDDZYBEQEDWQXZZBYKARQE

It was at that moment that my mind cleared as suddenly and completely as if someone had thrown a bucketful of water in my face. I jerked to my feet. The manager's chair fell back against the wall with a thud then slumped sideways on to the floor. I felt that had I fastened my hands on the desk I could have flung it headlong down the room. 'This is ridiculous!' I cried. 'This is absolute and sheer nonsense!'

The voices rose to a clamour within me. 'Sit down,' they were saying. 'Be quiet, stop arguing!' But anger carried me along as if on an irresistible tide. I knew for a fact that I had been duped. My hopes of freedom, raised perilously in the course of the day, were thrown down and smashed, apparently for ever. This creature into whose hands I had fallen, this Guide, had no intention of fulfilling his promises. I wasn't going to be free of the fatigue, the voices, the pain; as for the miraculous powers of healing, the wealth and prestige I was to enjoy as a reward for my sufferings, that was all a wild delusion.

'You liar!' I said, pounding my fist on the table. 'You miserable, wretched liar! How long have I believed your promises and obeyed you? And you never had the slightest intention of helping me. You charlatan! You villainous cheat! Well, just you wait. You've had it all your own way till now, but from here on it's all going to change. I'm going to − '

Suddenly I became aware of the silence around me. The jabbering of the voices had ceased. They seemed now to be listening attentively. I was reminded of the old gentleman at *Gossander*, standing with eyebrows raised, as if to say, 'Yes? And what is it you have to tell me?' I no more had an answer now than I had done then. What was I going to do to the Guide? What could I possibly do to him? My arms sank slowly down until they hung limply at my sides. There was absolutely nothing I could do. I was helpless.

The utter desperation of my plight began to dawn on me. Like a spy I had crept into the world of spirits and like a spy I had been taken prisoner there. Outwardly I had the appearance of freedom, but on the inside I had become a convict. The prospect of a life chained to the Guide and his friends stretched out ahead of me, seemingly without end. I had no doubt that my captors would take full advantage of my weakness. The torments, bad enough already, could only get worse. The nights would be more terrifying, sleep more scarce, my days increasingly lonely. At some stage I would crack. And what then? It didn't bear thinking about.

There was only one hope left. The Guide and his friends might be corrupt, but I could not believe the same was true of God. My instincts told me that he had to be just. How else could he run the universe? Furthermore he must necessarily be greater in authority and power than the Guide. I might be helpless, but not God. And hadn't I, in spite of all my mistakes, tried faithfully to trust and please him? Suddenly I cried out to God, the God whom for so long I had served. 'God, I know you're there. Please, please don't let me be tormented any longer. Let me be an ordinary person again, like Stan and the other people here. They're not tormented. I have tried to serve you, tried to do what you say, yet I'm in agony. I can't sleep. I can't do my job. Set me free. Please! I promise I'll do anything. Anything!'

I strained my ears in the silence. For a brief moment no reply came. Then, louder and clearer than I had ever heard it before, the voice returned. But it was not the same caressing voice of the Guide. It was a voice that seemed to rise out of chaos itself, a voice so horribly vicious and cruel that my spine froze at the sound of it. The words it spoke have ever since been burned on my consciousness:

'This isn't God. This is the Devil. And tonight I'm going to drive you mad!'

2: First encounter

'And who is the Devil, Mr Hartley?'

A sudden hush descended on the confirmation class. Twenty youngsters, sitting stiffly in the front pew of St George's Church, waited to see what Mr Hartley would do. The date was 18th March, 1928, a Sunday afternoon; the occasion, the fourth in a series of lectures preparatory to confirmation by the local bishop.

I was fourteen – a dark-haired, Northern youth with a strong rebellious streak. Given the choice I'd have been out playing football, not sitting on a hard wooden pew listening to the church warden. I was there, like everyone else, because my parents had wanted it. Confirmation was considered respectable in our neighbourhood even among the families that rarely, if ever, attended church. The children had to be 'done'. The fact that I was due to be done in a couple of weeks made the ordeal a bit more tolerable. At least after that I would be free to do as I liked.

There was one thing that softened my resistance to confirmation class – the fact that it was taken by Mr Hartley. I usually gave only grudging respect to my elders. Four years in a junior boys' boarding school had made me accustomed to tyranny. My father also was a stern disciplinarian, and kept a thick leather belt hanging on the kitchen door as a reminder of his power. But Mr Hartley never so much as raised his voice. In fact he had treated me from the very start as an equal, and thus won not only my respect but my attention. I was often able to suppress for quite a long time the desire to be doing something else, and listen with painful concentration to Mr Hartley's lectures. It was hard work: they were very dull.

He would pace back and forth between the pulpit and the font, murmuring his address, pausing occasionally to wipe his spectacles or jab a finger floorwards in support of his point. When in earnest his face would become a dark pink, contrasting sharply with the withered Edwardian sideburns. On these occasions his voice grew fainter and his expressions more obscure. But no one dared to interrupt him. We looked on humbly, feeling uncomfortable in our Sunday clothes, and wishing that four o'clock would roll round more quickly.

On this particular Sunday he had read to us a story from the Gospel of Matthew. The story perplexed me. Its old-fashioned language sounded very grand, but I didn't always understand what was meant. Jesus, it said, went into the wilderness and fasted for forty days, and 'he was afterward an hungred'. What could this mean? I decided on reflection that it must have wanted something to eat. Not surprising, after forty days without food! But what happened next was even stranger. The Devil turned up and invited him to transform the stones of the desert into loaves. This seemed quite a reasonable suggestion, since, as the writer pointed out, Jesus was the Son of God and could undoubtedly have done it had he wanted to. But Jesus was unmoved. He told the Devil that man was supposed to live on the words of God, not simply on bread.

The Devil then made a second suggestion, but rather less practical than the first. He took Jesus to the top of the temple roof and told him to throw himself off, for if he were really the Son of God, angels would then fly down to catch him. I didn't see much point in this. Neither did Jesus, apparently, because he replied curtly to the effect that the Devil had no business tempting him.

Undeterred, though, the Devil snatched Jesus from the temple roof and set him down instead on a very high mountain. From here every land in the world was visible. These, said the Devil, he would give to Jesus with only one string attached — that Jesus should get on his knees and worship him. On terms like those I myself would have been strongly tempted to accept. But Jesus only sent him away with the retort that God alone deserved worship, implying that if there were any worshipping to be done it was the Devil who should be doing it. With that the Devil left.

But who was the Devil? How did he have the power to make such fantastic offers, and why did he so much desire to be worshipped? His name, at least, was familiar to me. I remembered hearing in a reading from the Bible about a man 'possessed of the Devil' who was healed by Jesus. What could it be like, I wondered, for the Devil to possess you? The unpleasant sensations suggested by the phrase often crept over me when I talked to my grandmother, in whose conversation the Devil featured fairly prominently. He was usually called upon to enforce a threat; for instance, 'If you don't do such-and-such I'll tell the Devil to come and pinch you in the middle of the night'. The idea was sinister enough to make me comply with her wishes. But it also made me curious. A creature who did so many peculiar things must be worth investigating.

So I put my hand up and asked Mr Hartley.

I thought for a moment that I had made a terrible mistake, for the old gentleman stopped in his tracks and drew his brows together in a frown. It was not considered polite in any church function to interrupt the speaker. The same question asked in the same circumstances of the Rector would certainly have drawn down wrath. My friend Peter who was sitting next to me elbowed me in the ribs. I felt my face redden. But I needn't have worried, for Mr Hartley never frowned from displeasure, only from a tender concern that he should be understood.

After what seemed like a very long time he cleared his throat and said, 'Well, Robert, that's a very important question. But perhaps we should ask first of all, not *who* he is, but *whether* he is'

He had lost me here. 'Yes,' I replied, mechanically.

'For instance, have you ever met the Devil?'

'I don't think so.'

'And do you know anyone who has?'

'My gran might have done. She talks about him a lot.'

There were shuffles next to me in the pew. Everyone found this amusing. Mr Hartley smiled and went on, 'Well, I'm probably as old as your grandmother, and I've never met the Devil. This is the problem, you see. No one can actually prove that the Devil exists. There are many stories about him, like the one we've just read. But you can't go and see him as you could, say, Stanley Baldwin or the Rector. And if something can't be proved we should be very careful before believing it.'

27

'You mean there's really no such person as the Devil?'

'No more, I think, than there was a talking serpent in the Garden of Eden.'

This possibility had never occurred to me. My interest had been aroused to such a pitch that I would have been willing to believe all sorts of things about the Devil. To be told flatly that he didn't exist was rather an anticlimax.

'But why write about a serpent or a Devil when neither of them exists?' I said at last.

'It's just a way of speaking,' replied Mr Hartley. 'I'm sure that the writers of Genesis and of Matthew's Gospel didn't really believe in an evil person called the Devil. But in both cases they wanted to show that the principal character − Eve in the first case and Jesus in the second − was being tempted by *sin*. Now sin is real, and temptation is real, but neither is very easy to imagine. Suppose, for instance, that the writer of Matthew had pictured Jesus being tempted by "sin". Would you have found it as easy to understand the story?'

I had to shake my head. The term 'sin' meant absolutely nothing to me.

'Well, then,' said Mr Hartley, his complexion turning a shade rosier, 'it couldn't have worked, could it? It's far too hard for a reader to imagine "sin" tempting Christ with the kingdoms of the world. Sin doesn't speak, it has no body. So instead of talking about sin in the abstract the writer turns it into a person − he personifies it. He thinks, "What would sin look like if it were in a body, and what name would it have?" And so he invents the Devil.'

'But isn't he telling a lie?' I persisted.

'Not really. He's just telling the truth in a way that's easier to understand. I'm sure that no one today would consider that Jesus actually spoke to someone in the wilderness. It's ridiculous. There are all sorts of things in the Bible about the supernatural − angels, miracles and so forth − that can't possibly be true. Science has disproved them. The only reason they're there in the Gospels is that the writers wanted to make their point more forcefully. In the twentieth century we don't have to take it all as literal truth. What nonsense! We must see through the references to the supernatural and get to the real teaching.'

I only half understood this argument, but it had a sense of finality about it that deeply impressed me. I wondered what Gran would have made of it. With a smug look on my face I replied, 'My gran says the Devil is bright red with a pointed tail, and puts stones in your shoe if you don't do what she says.'

'Then your gran needs to be confirmed,' retorted Mr Hartley in a rare turn of wit.

This was so unexpected that the whole class broke out in a fit of snickering. It was snickering and not outright laughter because to laugh in church was thought out of place; but all the girls looked down into their laps and the boys, including Peter, exchanged smiles. A joke from Mr Hartley was history in the making.

When we were quiet again Mr Hartley went back to his lecture. Picking up his battered leather Bible and fixing me with his eye he said, 'The *real* point of the story, you see, has nothing to do with the Devil. What the writer means us to learn is ... '

Sin. No topic existed on which Mr Hartley waxed more eloquent or to which he returned with greater frequency. We never found out what it was (Mr Hartley never defined it), but of the direness of its consequences we were left in no doubt. Sin spelled ruination for anyone unfortunate enough to stumble across it. Week after week he would unearth the subject and repeat its moral, closing with the formula, 'Whatever you do, young people, *don't* ... " On this Sunday his audience paid more attention than usual. Even Peter listened after the crack about my grandmother. But my mind was elsewhere.

My eyes had drifted off Mr Hartley to the window at the end of the chancel. Here was depicted the celebrated battle between St George and the dragon. The saint, in claret armour and seated on a rearing white stallion, was dealing the death-blow to his victim. The dragon lay curled beneath the charger's hoofs, casting one last, venomous glance up at his assailant before the sword fell.

The picture had always fascinated me, partly because of the richness of its colours and partly because the dragon reminded me of the Devil. Today it took on a symbolic significance. Mr Hartley seemed to have killed off the Devil just as St George was killing the dragon in the window. I tried to imagine Mr Hartley with his white whiskers clad in armour and swinging the long, sharp sword, and almost laughed again, it was so ridiculous. Yet the conviction with which he had dismissed the Devil had made an impact on me. Angels, miracles – all the extraordinary things I had never dreamed of challenging – were swept aside in an instant: science had disproved them. Science was certainly a mighty sword to wield. Could it really do all these things? I felt all of a sudden that the axe had been laid at the roots of a very large tree. The whole edifice of my childhood beliefs shuddered under the blows.

At last Mr Hartley finished his lecture and we all stood up to recite the creed and the Lord's Prayer. That would normally have presaged our dismissal, but just as we were picking up our books there came the sound of footsteps in the aisle behind us. They echoed off the tiles like water dripping in a cave. We looked round to see the Rector approaching.

He reached the front and with a slight nod to Mr Hartley wheeled round to face us. He was a tall man; he commanded respect because he could look down on people, and because of the severe expression that inevitably came to his face while he was doing it. He surveyed us coolly.

'Good afternoon, boys and girls.'

'Good afternoon, sir.' We chimed.

'I hope you are enjoying your lessons with the warden?'

'Yes, sir.'

'How are they doing, Mr Hartley?'

'Satisfactorily, Reverend.'

The Rector's mouth curled into a smile, which then vanished without trace. He went on, 'My reason for seeing you is to remind you all of the Bishop's visit next week. It is the Bishop's duty to ensure that you are being adequately taught' (he glanced at Mr Hartley), 'and, of course, he wants to meet you all before you go forward for confirmation. That means you must take extra care with your appearance. We don't want to give St George's a bad name, do we?'

'No, sir.'

'Very well. That is all.'

Mr Hartley gave the signal and we rose to go out. The Rector observed us silently, but when I reached the end of the pew he called me over to him. He looked at me critically before asking my name.

'Robert Lee, sir,' I replied.

'Lee. Yes, your father looks after the electricity, doesn't he?'

'Yes, sir. He's chief officer in the borough.'

'He's a good man. A pity we don't see more of him at St George's.'

I didn't know how to reply to this. I felt as if I were being made responsible for my father's absence. That was hardly fair – he wouldn't have come if I'd pleaded for it. I swallowed uncomfortably.

'I don't know why he doesn't come, sir,' I said.

'It would be a credit to him if he did. Make sure you invite him to the confirmation service. It's an important day when a boy is confirmed. Tell him I should like to introduce the Bishop to him.'

'Yes, sir.'

'Do you know your catechism yet?'

'I'm learning it, sir.'

'Good. You can be on your way now.'

I walked down towards the west door of the church. The Rector must have been watching me go, because there was no sound behind me. He seemed to watch everyone as if they were insects crawling around under a magnifying glass – everyone with a social position inferior to his own, that is. Bishops and local luminaries occupied rungs above him; ordinary parishioners, children and church wardens were definitely below. I often felt a pang of resentment at his treatment of Mr Hartley, whom I would have classed as a far better man. And to be questioned about my father, over whose habits I had no control, then prodded about my catechism, made me positively angry. Learning the catechism was for me a cruel and unnecessary torture. Why rectors couldn't get people confirmed without it I simply didn't know.

Peter was waiting for me outside. We set off together through the graveyard, a crisp spring breeze blowing in our faces.

'What did he want?' said Peter.

'Asking about Father. He's cross because Father won't go to church.'

'My dad won't, neither. So what's the difference?'

The difference was one of status. Peter's family lived at the bottom end of the hill.

'That was a good one Hartley pulled about your gran', Peter continued. 'Were you telling the truth about her saying the Devil puts stones in your shoe?'

'Oh, yes. She says that sort of thing all the time.'

'Do you believe her?'

'Course not.'

'Bet you do. You wouldn't have asked Hartley about the Devil, otherwise.'

'I don't,' I protested. 'I was just curious.'

Peter gave me a knowing smile.

'What do you think about it, then,' I said.

'About the Devil? Hartley's right. There isn't a Devil. But there isn't a God, neither.'

'How do you know that?'

'My brother's in the Navy. He's been to all sorts of foreign countries where they worship statues and trees. Everybody's got their own God, he says.'

'But don't you think there's a real God − a big one.?'

'Nah,' drawled Peter.

We were now at the crest of the hill and looking down over the town centre. Stockport wasn't the prettiest town in Cheshire. Its chimneys poked out of the earth like soot-caked fingers. Some of them seemed to have been lopped off at the knuckle, and others to have grown out to an unnatural length. Beneath them lay the black, ordered ranks of industrial housing, broken here and there by a road or a stretch of derelict land.

'See over there, next to the river?' said Peter, pointing. 'That's where I work.' He searched and pointed to another building, a drab one with dark slate roof. 'And that's the Grammar.'

I gazed down glumly. The next morning I would be under that roof, labouring behind my desk in what my father considered the best school in town, and hating every minute of it. I envied Peter. He had left the previous year and started work. It wasn't a good job; he was just running errands in an office, and in this depressed region he was lucky to be doing that. But it was a job, and he was free, which was more than I could say of myself. I lived for the day when I'd be able to leave school for ever and be out earning money.

We stood silently for a few moments. Somewhere in the town below a bell tolled five o'clock.

'I'm going to be late,' I said.

We went to the corner where the road divided, and Peter ran off down the hill. My road climbed gently round the hillside. Walking at a smart pace I arrived home in five minutes. We lived in a very respectable part of town called Davenport. The house, *Kintra,* spacious by the standards of the area, was a contrast to the humble cottage on Hall Street where I'd been born. I loved it. The garden was broad and grass-covered and was ideal for punting a ball about or playing tag with my sister Jo. I went in and hung my cap on the peg. My mother was in the kitchen, supervising the maid. Like many successful Northern families we had a housekeeper in residence. She saw me standing in the doorway.

'Ah, there you are. I thought you'd never come.'

'Sorry, Mother. The Rector wanted to talk to me.'

'Did he now? Well, I suppose that's a good excuse.' She turned to the maid. 'Annie, go and tell Bob that Max is home.'

Bob was my father. Since we were both called Robert, I was known in the family as Max – my middle name.

I followed my mother into the dining-room, where tea was already on the table. Jo joined us, and we stood behind our seats until Father and Gran came in. My father was in his forties, a lean-featured man with dark, well-oiled hair. He was rarely seen about the house without his pipe, even when it wasn't lit. He laid it down next to him as he sat down. I tried to work out whether he was in a good mood. He wasn't the sort to fly into an uncontrollable temper, but there was no telling when I had earned his disapproval, and if I had, I would need to watch my step.

We started to eat. It was my mother who spoke first.

'Max has been talking with the Rector, Bob.'

My father, who had his mouth full, raised his eyebrows. 'And what did the Rector say to him?'

'What did the Rector say, Max?'

I mumbled my reply.

'Speak up,' said my father.

'He said he'd like to introduce the Bishop to you, Father.'

'Ah.' He lifted a slice of cold pork on to his plate and started to tease off the fat with the knife. 'And when does the Bishop hope to be granted this pleasure?'

'At the confirmation service, I think. The Rector said to make sure I invited you.'

My father smiled in the fashion of a chess player who has just made a winning move. 'So. The Rector wants me in church.'

'He's right, Bob,' my mother broke in, 'we ought to be seen there just occasionally, especially if our Max here is being done. It'll make a good impression. Now, Max, don't you worry. You tell the Rector, of course your father and I will be there. It will be an honour to meet the Bishop.'

'An honour to meet the Bishop,' mimicked my father. 'Honestly, Meg, have some self-respect. The Bishop, apparently, is more eager to meet us than we are to meet him. You can tell the Rector, Max, that we will be there if our commitments permit us to.'

I looked at my parents each in turn. 'Yes, Father,' I said.

My grandmother, who was sitting opposite me in her habitual, black frock, intervened. 'How's your old friend Mr Hartley, then?' she said.

'He's looking well, Gran.'

'And are you learning your lessons?'

'He never learns his lessons,' said my father, with asperity.

Mother reprimanded him. 'There's no good talking like that in the boy's hearing, Bob.'

'It's true, and it needs to be said,' my father insisted. 'Look at the money we paid for him to study at Bastion House. I thought at least that would toughen him up a bit. Evidently I was wrong. And now that I've got him into the Grammar he's doing just as badly there.'

I stared down at my plate. I had loathed Bastion House from start to finish. It was a small boarding school at Caernarfon, on the north coast of Wales. The whole place had only one heater. All three classes, the juniors, middle school and seniors, were taught in a single room. The headmaster and his daughter, who presided at opposite ends of the room, spent half their time yelling at each other to keep quiet. I had no pretences to being a genius, but a place like that would have spoilt the most promising candidate. By the time I got to Stockport Grammar I was two years behind in my studies.

'I never liked Bastion House,' I said miserably.

'Never liked it!' said my father. 'Some people never get the change to go to any school. My father certainly couldn't afford to

34

send me. I got to where I am by slogging my way up from the shop-floor. Instead of studying I was lighting boilers in Darwen power-station. I didn't have any fancy qualifications to give me promotion. The trouble with you, boy, is that you're too choosy. If you'd had more guts you'd have sailed through Bastion House with no trouble at all.'

'Bob, there's no need to be vulgar,' my mother pleaded.

But by this time my little sister Jo was ready to join in the fun. 'Yes,' she said to me, 'It's like that morning Mr Davies took the school down for a swim in the sea, and you were so scared you locked yourself in the toilet!'

'And the same goes for you,' said my mother, sternly.

'That's precisely what I mean,' my father said. 'No guts.'

'Oh, Bob, give the boy a chance. It was the middle of January, and you know yourself how bad his chest is. He'll do all right. He just needs a bit of help, don't you, Max?'

She patted my hand affectionately. Father had shoved his plate away with a scornful gesture and was knocking on the table with his pipe. I looked down at my half-eaten cold potatoes and salad and realised I had lost my appetite. Arguments at mealtimes always gave me a queasy stomach. Sighing, I replaced the knife and fork. Gran immediately hissed at me across the table, and looking down I discovered with horror that I had put them back in reverse, as if I were left-handed. I switched them quickly.

'Two months' bad luck,' said Gran in a hoarse whisper.

My mother and Jo were staring at me in dismay. I bit my lip. Few of us went to church, but when it came to superstition the Lees were the most religious family in Stockport. Even my father, who paid less attention than the womenfolk to such things as ladders, salt and broken mirrors, was not immune to it. A wry smile came to his face. 'That's till the eighteenth of May,' he said.

'Don't be like that, Bob,' said my mother. 'Anyone can have bad luck. It's not so terrible. Besides, they say bad luck is far less effective if you remember to say your prayers. You always say your prayers, don't you, Max?'

'Yes, Mother.'

'And it's true, isn't it, Gran, about prayers and luck?'

But Gran's face was set like stone.

'There!' said my mother, rallying, 'What did I tell you? Everything's going to be all right.' She smoothed my hair with her hand and smiled warmly at me.

The rest of the meal passed with conversation about our relatives. There was always some scandal to be chewed over and condemned. Today's concerned a distant cousin of mine who was to be married rather more quickly than was decent for a girl in her teens. Added spice was to be found in the fact that at my age she had been a keen church-goer. I dimly recollected her. On her brief and infrequent visits to Stockport she had broken a good number of my toys. I listened for a while. Gran was at her best on topics like this. But I had no more appetite for it than I had for the food, and I was glad when Father rose and took his pipe back into the drawing-room. I asked to be excused, and went out for a walk.

I felt angry. Angry at the Rector for his high-handedness and his demand that I should learn a lot of religious rules that were never going to do me any good; angry at my father for complaining about my performance at school. No one seemed to take *my* views into consideration. Why did I have to go through confirmation just because the adults thought I should? Why couldn't I go out to work instead of toiling away at the Grammar and suffering my father's disdain because I didn't make the grade? Both of them would have done better with someone else instead of me. There must have been a boy somewhere who actually enjoyed the catechism. Why not pick on him? And my father had virtually said to my face that I was a disappointment to him as a son. That hurt me. But if it was true he might have the decency to stop expecting me to fulfil his expectations.

In the past my father's coldness had always driven me to my mother. She was by nature a sympathetic person: it was she who had relieved the discomfort of living at Bastion House by sending me a weekly food parcel. But this evening she, too, had made me angry. I was reaching the age when a mother's attentions, especially when given in public, caused me shame instead of consolation. I felt I ought to be standing up for myself, not hiding behind her all the time.

And then there was the luck. For as long as I could remember I had been entangled in this web of family lore. Good and bad luck were part of my world, however strenuously I might deny it to Peter. My present mood was to a considerable degree the result of having received back luck over dinner. I resented being sentenced in this way. Luck was a sort of club with which the family seemed to beat me when I displeased them. And the only way I could escape the bad luck when I'd got it was to say my prayers – an arduous routine I went through before bed which seemed to have lost all purpose beyond being a sort of insurance policy against misfortune. The whole weary cycle made me fed up.

By now I had reached the hill crest where Peter and I had stood before dinner. The wind had dropped, and the smoke from hundreds of kitchen fires was settling in a blanket over the town. A single star was visible on the far horizon. My mind drifted back to the class at St George's and what Mr Hartley had told me about the Devil. The Devil seemed to be the cornerstone of the family's religious beliefs, such as they were. Could it really be true that he didn't exist? There was something very attractive about believing that. It undermined all the superstition that I hated so much yet was unable to break free from. It was a sort of secret revenge. I wanted that. I wanted some way of asserting myself and getting my own back. That would make me feel that I wasn't, after all, the failure my father took me for; and who could tell – one day I might be able to prove it.

When the light faded I turned for home. The electric lamps my father had introduced in Stockport formed a thread of lights up the street. I followed them to the front door, and went in. On the landing I met my mother. She had just put Jo to bed and was on her way down to the drawing-room for coffee. She drew my lips to hers for a kiss. 'Good-night, dear,' she said, softly, 'and don't forget your prayers.'

'No, Mother.'

I paused to watch her go down the stairs, then washed, and entered my bedroom. My Bible and prayer book were lying on the table where I'd left them the night before. I looked at them, and then let my gaze drop to the floor. I went straight to bed.

3: Ghosts

Almost thirty years later to the day I went to see *Hamlet*.

For a long time after my small act of defiance over the prayers nothing had really changed. But in the early 1930s Father earned another promotion, this time to a job in London. This caused me immense relief, since I would be obliged to leave Stockport Grammar and be unable to take the matriculation, which I would almost certainly have failed. My father's next proposal was that I should attend London County Council evening classes. I held out little more hope for this than I had for Bastion House or the grammar school. It promised to be yet another ruinous chapter in my father's mismanagement of my life. So I rebelled.

I set out on the far more ambitious path of becoming a chartered electrical engineer. The course, offered at Regent Street Polytechnic, was of five years' duration. It took me eight years. But I graduated successfully just before the place closed down at the outbreak of the Second World War. The qualification helped to exempt me from military service, and I spent the war years keeping the power supplies going during the blitz in East London. I worked like a beaver, on the job by day and in my study at night. I had never before enjoyed such a sense of self-esteem. I really thought I'd made it.

It was during the war that I married Joanna, a pretty brunette I'd fallen in love with at the Poly. The service was held at the Queen's Chapel of the Savoy. The day was unusual because not a single German bomb fell on the city while we were there. After the war we settled down in the London suburb of Barking, with our first two children, Jill and Bob, and for the next fourteen years led a quiet and very happy family life.

At the same time I was making steady progress through the ranks of the power industry. It was much the same sort of progress as my father had made a generation before, from small beginnings to a comfortable prosperity. He had even been awarded an MBE before his death. I liked to think that, although our relationship had never grown to be a warm one, I might have given him some cause for pride. My latest promotion had been made public only a few days ago, and it was to celebrate it that Joanna and I had gone to the West End for dinner and a visit to the theatre.

We drove back through the city centre, chatting in a light-hearted way about the production of this great Shakespearean tragedy. It started, of course, with the old king's ghost. He had stood in a sea of stage-smoke, in full battle dress but as pale as a marble statue. The scene was well managed. It wouldn't have been too hard to believe that he was a real ghost. That set turning in my mind a few wheels that had been motionless for a very long time.

'You know,' I said to Joanna, 'My father once saw a ghost. At least he said he did.'

'I can't imagine your father confessing to something like that. Who's ghost was it?'

'Pemmie, Uncle Albert's wife.'

'I don't recall either of them.'

'No. They both died long before you arrived on the scene. Albert wasn't a real uncle.'

'No uncles are.'

I chuckled. 'Oh, I had a few. Like Uncle Will. He was the one in cotton. He always used to say to me, "Max, if every Chinaman would only wear his shirt an inch longer I'd be in work for years." '

Joanna laughed. 'And what about Uncle Albert?'

'His real name was Gardiner. Worked as a rep for Baxendales. I never saw him without a cigarette in his mouth. But he was a jolly old soul – I suppose that's why my father liked him. Father felt he was misunderstood at home. Mother, in her good-natured way, was always telling him off. So he spent as much time as he could with friends. Albert and he got along like a house on fire, though it's hard to imagine it. Albert usually wore a white suit and shoes, just like he owned a plantation in the tropics. And, well, you know how conservative Father was.'

'So when did he see the ghost?'

'That must have been sometime during the Depression. It was Christmas. Pemmie died quite suddenly on Christmas Eve. Albert, of course, was devastated. A general emergency was declared, and Father went over to sit through the night with him. I must say I've never had a Christmas go off as much like a damp squib as that one did. The worst thing was Father's face when he came home the next morning. He was as white as my collar.

We sat him down and all crowded round to listen. And for a bit he just said, "That's the most frightening experience I've ever had." It was murder waiting for him to continue. We couldn't imagine what had happened. In the end he told us he'd been sitting in front of the fire with Albert when all of a sudden the door opened and in walked Pemmie's ghost. She didn't seem to notice Father. She just went over to Albert, bent down and kissed him on the head. At which point Albert cried, "She kissed me! She kissed me!" Father, I think, was about ready to throw himself out of the window.'

'How awful!'

'It must have been ten times worse for Albert. He was bald.'

Joanna giggled. 'You shouldn't make fun of him. It isn't very pleasant being bereaved.'

'Oh, he soon bounced back. The next Christmas he was his normal self, and married to a much younger woman called Edith.'

We drove on in silence for a while. But there was more going on in my mind than anecdotes about my Uncle Albert. It wasn't long before I said, 'I've never seen a ghost. Have you?'

'No,' said Joanna. But she must have picked up that the question was serious, because she looked at me and asked, 'What's on your mind?'

'I'm not sure.'

There was another pause, then I said, 'Doesn't your mother know something about them?'

'She's a spiritist.'

'That's it. Tell me about it.'

'I don't know very much. Mummy used to be a regular at the

40

local spiritist church, so she could tell you more. I think there's usually a medium there, and messages for people. Friends and relatives and the like.'

'Dead ones?'

'Yes. They say what it's like on the other side, reassure you. It's all very rational, really. There's our world, and another one, another dimension if you like, where we go when we die. The Greeks knew about it. They called it Hades.'

'Have you ever been to a meeting?'

'I used to go with Mummy a lot when I was young. I kind of got out of the habit. I don't think I've been once since we got married. It doesn't matter much. The spiritists don't expect you to be there every week.'

'Not like ordinary churches,' I said. We were approaching Oxford Street. I turned into Kingsway, peering at the buildings on my left. 'There,' I said, pointing. 'They're the worst.' Passing by on Joanna's side was a large Catholic church. I had noticed it many times when I had worked in the area during the war. 'Hypocrites,' I went on. 'The lot of them. We've got a few at the office. They go to confession on Sundays, then booze themselves to oblivion for the rest of the week.'

Joanna looked at it but made no reply.

'You know, I'd like to visit a spiritist church,' I said. 'I'm curious to find out what goes on.'

'What's behind all this, Robert?' said Joanna suddenly.

I thought for a moment before replying.

'It goes back a long way. When I was about fourteen my father decided I should be confirmed. That was shortly after he sent me to Stockport Grammar School. Neither decision, I think, was very sensible. But at the class I had to attend before being confirmed I met an old man called Mr Hartley. A real saint. I wouldn't mind if all church-goers were like him. I remember one Sunday we had a discussion about the Devil. Of course, having Gran around I had come to believe all sorts of superstitious nonsense about the Devil. But Mr Hartley said something like, "The thing with the Devil is not who he is, but whether he is." '

I smiled. 'I like that. You see, Mr Hartley's point was that no one could prove that the Devil existed. Hence there was no use in believing he did. Eventually I came to the conclusion that what applied to the Devil applied also to superstition and to God – in fact to the whole of the supernatural. I couldn't prove God or the afterlife; they never did anything useful for me. So I gave up believing in them. Simple as that.'

I paused, staring ahead into the city lights. 'But I think I may have been wrong. Not about the Church – the Christian faith is too far-fetched and the people who practise it are soft in the head. All religions are full of cranks and hypocrites. But just because religion is wrong doesn't mean there's no such thing as an afterlife. After all, people have been seeing ghosts since the Stone Age. People who have no religious beliefs whatever have seen them. In my book that implies that religion and the afterlife are quite separate things, and that the best way to approach the supernatural is to prove it scientifically. Proof should be easy enough to obtain. All you need do is some careful observation. Go to a seance, for instance, and see whether the messages are authentic. You'd soon find out if the thing was rigged. Do you see?'

I glanced at Joanna. 'Yes, I suppose so,' she said. 'But it seems like an awful lot of bother.'

'Oh, come on! Look, why don't we make a proper investigation of spiritism, you and me, and prove whether there's anything in it or not?'

'All right,' said Joanna, suppressing a yawn.

'Right, then. Let's drop by that spiritist church tonight on our way home and find out what time the service is on Sunday. It's somewhere near here, isn't it?'

'Robert, do we have to go right now?'

'Why not?'

'Because I'm tired and I want to go to bed.'

'It won't take five minutes.'

We turned right and soon after stopped the car in a turning by the church. It was late now. A few stragglers were drifting out of the pubs after closing time, hugging their coats and blowing cold puffs of steam into the night air. I shoved one hand into my pocket and put the other round Joanna's waist. We walked down the dimly lit street without speaking. The spiritist church stood on its own in front of a car park, a long, low building with double doors opening on to the pavement. It was in total darkness, with no sign of life.

'This is it,' I said, examining the sign above the doors.

'Hurry up, then. It's cold.'

I stepped forward to look at the notice board, then gave a start. There was a man standing in the doorway. All I saw at first was the tip of his cigarette, which glowed brightly as he drew on it and dropped down with the motion of his hand. But now, as he stirred, shifting from one foot to the other, I caught an impression of his face; it was slender, with hollow cheeks and a brow prominent enough to keep the eyes from view. He seemed to be gazing at the buildings across the street. He was, at least, completely unperturbed by my arrival.

'I'm sorry,' I said, 'I didn't see you there.'

'Don't worry.'

He didn't offer to get out of the way, so I said, 'I don't know if you can help me. My wife and I wanted to come to a service at this church.'

'There's no more services here tonight.'

'No, well, when's the next one?'

He paused a long time before answering. He seemed almost unwilling to tell me. At length he said, 'Sunday. If you come back Sunday at six o'clock you'll catch the service.'

'Thank you. And are you a member of the church?'

'After a fashion ... '

He threw the stub of his cigarette on to the pavement and crushed it under his foot, then proceeded to walk away. I called out 'Thanks!' but he didn't turn round.

'What an odd fellow,' I said, returning to Joanna.

'Just a wanderer.'

'But he implied he was a member of the congregation.'

'Perhaps he was the caretaker or something. That would make sense. He probably locked the place up, then stopped for a smoke before going home.'

I shrugged. 'Perhaps. All the same, you'd expect him to be a bit more welcoming. It almost seemed as if he would have preferred us not to come.'

'Caretakers are funny types.'

'Well, at least we know when the place opens on Sunday. I dare say we'll meet him again then.'

But we didn't. When we came back on Sunday evening I was stepping into a group of complete strangers. The congregation totalled about forty, predominantly women in their sixties and seventies. We stood around at the back of the hall. I heard snatches of conversation about husbands and sickness and healing 'by spirit'. The general tone was hushed and expectant.

Eventually we were greeted by the President, a man of about my age but thinner and a shade taller. He had lost much of his hair and what remained was combed elaborately sideways to disguise his baldness. He had acquired the habit of passing his hand back over his scalp, to check that things were still in place. After a short and awkward conversation he excused himself on the grounds of having to arrange the chairs.

He convened the meeting promptly at half-past six. I let everyone else go forward first and placed myself in a strategic position near the back. Now I had the chance to look at it I noticed that the hall, though referred to as a church, was very unlike any church I had ever seen. The use of chairs for pews was one obvious difference. Another was the conspicuous absence of decoration. There were no stained-glass windows, and in place of an altar there was a table with a vase of flowers on top.

On one side of the table sat the President; on the other the visiting medium, whom he introduced as Mrs Rose Dawson. She was, he said, a woman of 'exceptional gifts'. She had kindly consented to speak tonight even though she lived in Slough, and would of course be giving the customary demonstrations of her art. Most of the old ladies nodded at this. Mrs Dawson, a matronly figure in a pink and flame-yellow evening dress, gave a confident smile.

The service began with a hymn entitled 'How strange it is on the farther shore', accompanied on the organ. Mrs Dawson's voice was clearly audible above the rest: many of the elder members weren't singing, and I was too busy observing people to follow the words.

The President then gave the readings, one from the Bible, the other from a spiritist writer I'd never heard of. Nobody seemed to be paying much attention. I got the feeling that these were preliminaries, and everyone was waiting for the 'real' service to begin. I judged that this happened when Mrs Dawson rose to speak. There was a quick shuffling of seats followed by intense silence.

The medium stood forward, holding a sheaf of notes as a bridesmaid might hold a bouquet, and addressed the congregation loudly on the topic of spiritual perfection. It was, I thought, a competent talk spoilt by its archaisms. She had a tendency when excited to lapse into Shakespearean English, putting 'hath' for 'has', 'doth' for 'does', and introducing her opinions with a studied 'methinks'. But no one else seemed to mind. The old women in particular muttered in agreement at her scoldings and sighed lavishly when she became sentimental. After a dramatic conclusion she retired amid murmurs of 'Wonderful!' and Bless you, dear!'

At this point the President rose. He thanked Mrs Dawson and turned to us. 'Now we've reached the last part of our service,' he said. 'It's what we call the "Proof of Survival". Mrs Dawson told me when she came in that there are strong vibrations here. So let's concentrate on producing those vibrations while our medium listens for the spirits.'

Everyone sat very still. Some had closed their eyes, others were staring at the floor. Quietly, I slipped a notepad from my pocket and opened it at the first page. For a while there was complete silence. I could hear the moan of traffic on the high road outside. I had never attended a meeting like this before, and it gave me a slightly eerie sensation.

The first thing the medium said was, 'I'm getting a picture – a soldier in uniform. And a word, too. Does "amputee" mean anything to anyone?'

'Yes!'

I jumped, because the woman who spoke was right next to me. 'Yes, that's my husband,' she said. 'He lost his leg at Dieppe during the war.'

'Now I'm getting names. Billie, and Charles.'

'Billie, yes, that's my uncle. Charles was my grandfather.'

I glanced up. The woman had her eyes shut tight. She was straining forward on her seat, smiling euphorically.

'Mary,' said the medium.

This time the woman didn't answer, but I could see she was thinking hard. Someone said, 'Bless you'. There were murmurs of encouragement from all over the room.

'I've got the soldier again. He has medals, and a rifle. He's very close to you now. You will feel his face against your cheek.'

The woman sighed. I looked round instinctively, but there was no ghostly form stooping next to her's. Just the woman, quivering slightly. 'Yes, yes,' she said, 'I feel him.'

'I give you a handful of poppies,' said the medium, throwing her arms wide. 'Go and put them on his grave.'

The poppies must have been symbolic, because there were no poppies on the table, and Mrs Dawson certainly hadn't lobbed any into the congregation. I scribbled down the details of the case. Meanwhile Mrs Dawson was receiving another picture.

'Rheumatism. In the hips.'

Nobody replied immediately. I guessed that several people present suffered from this complaint. They needed more to go on.

'A tall lady with a blue veil.'

'My mother,' said one of the women in the front row.

'Herbs. Does that mean anything to you?'

'Yes. My mother always used them for medicine.'

'She was right. They are the proper thing to use. There are no drugs in the world of spirit.' Mrs Dawson paused. 'I see a blue healing light. It is descending on you. Your aura is very bright: it is surrounding the lower part of your body. Do you feel the heat?'

'Yes,' said the woman. 'It's tingly, like pins and needles.'

'That's the healing light at work. Your mother's vibrations are strong. She's saying you must rest for the next two weeks to let the healing take effect.'

I noted this case, too. It was easy enough to verify. I could ask the woman whether the healing had been effective or not. If it was, that was evidence in favour of the medium. If not, I would have good reason to call it a hoax. The woman was sitting a few rows in front of me, and her head was obscured. I peered through the congregation, trying to see something that would help me recognise her. The medium had started speaking again.

'There is a tall man here, at the back. He has never been before. He is wearing a green sports coat.'

Several people looked round. I sat, sucking the end of my pencil, momentarily lost in thought.

'He has many relatives on the other side, I know,' said Mrs Dawson.

The two old ladies sitting immediately in front of me turned round, whispering loudly. I put a stroke under the last line I had written and glanced up. In two seconds the truth had dawned.

Mrs Dawson was talking to *me*.

My first reaction was to slap the pencil on to the notepad and smother both with my hands, just as if I'd been caught scratching graffiti on my desk at school. My heart began to race. I looked up at Mrs Dawson, who was on her feet, her eyes closed and arms stretched out towards me.

'I am getting very strong vibrations from you, sir. Are you a healer?'

'No,' I stuttered.

'That is very strange. Very strange. I am getting an old man with white hair. Do you know who it is?'

By now I was recovering myself a bit. I replied, 'No. It could be anybody.'

'He is very old and very wise. He is talking to you. One word keeps coming to me – *decision*. You have made a decision. He says it is the right one; you should not go back on it, but what you need is commitment.'

For a few seconds Mrs Dawson fell silent, her face set in an attitude of intense concentration. Then she said, 'Your vibrations are incredibly strong. I cannot leave you. Are you sure you have no power to heal?'

'I've never tried it,' I said.

'Aaah! There is much for you to do in the world of spirit. I give you – I give you a signpost!'

Mrs Dawson then subsided into her chair. There were two or three more messages much in the style of the others, after which the President closed with a prayer to the spirits who had been with us for the evening. It all seemed to pass very quickly. I hardly listened to the other messages, I was so taken up with my own. I kept on turning it over in my mind, squeezing out the last ounce of significance.

My overriding response was one of suspicion. There had been little so far in this meeting to convince a sceptic like me that these messages really *were* coming from the supernatural world. The medium could easily have picked up a few helpful hints from the President before the show began. He would know, for instance, if a member's husband had lost his leg at Dieppe. It was equally possible that Joanna's mother had given him some details about me. If so, I wasn't going to be duped that easily. At the same time I had to admit that the message had pierced the mental armour with which I was defending myself. It had entered at a level where my reason was powerless to prevent it, and its barbs had stuck. I felt surprised, even flattered, that I should be thought to have such exceptional abilities to heal.

There was a scraping of seats as people got up. The President reminded the congregation that tea would be served as usual, and that the next meeting would be the mid-week seance. I decided to seize the opportunity and talk to Mrs Dawson. No one else had approached her, probably because her brazen manner made her rather intimidating. I introduced myself.

'Ah, the man in the green sports coat!' she responded, parting her brightly painted lips in a grin.

I took her hand. 'The man with the vibrations, you mean.'

'Remarkable,' she said, gravely, 'absolutely remarkable. I've never seen anything like it.'

'I'm afraid I'm sceptical.'

'Are you? What a pity.'

'Well, no one can see these vibrations, least of all me. With respect, you might be taking me for a ride.'

'Ah, but can you see love, or truth, or justice?'

'I can see their effects,' I said shortly. 'If vibrations have any effect I haven't noticed it yet.'

'But you will, if you try. You see, everyone has some psychic potential, but in some it is stunted, latent. Now your potential is tremendous. You've had it from childhood, I'm sure. What you must do now is bring it out, let it develop.'

'Which is why I need "commitment"?'

'Absolutely!' cried Mrs Dawson, ignoring the hint of sarcasm in my voice. 'You mustn't turn back now. It would be a crime. The spirits are telling you to go on and be a healer. You don't realise what a service you can perform for mankind. You have decided to come here tonight. That was the right decision. Don't go back on it.'

I laughed. 'I'm sorry,' I said. 'That's all very well, but the only decision I've made is to investigate spiritism, to find out whether there really is an afterlife or a God or whatever. I'm not satisfied yet that any of them exist. You can't expect me to throw myself into being a healer if I don't believe in spirits.'

Mrs Dawson took a sip of tea, leaving a crimson smudge of lipstick on the rim of the cup, and said with an air of assurance,

'Well, you won't know until you try. If the Proofs of Survival didn't persuade you (and with a man who has a mind as strong as yours I can well believe it) then perhaps you should attend a seance or, better still, approach the spirits on your own.'

'Become a medium, you mean?'

'Not straight away. A good way to start is to get yourself a ouija board.'

'Never heard of it.'

'It used to be called a planchette board. It has numbers and letters printed on it, and a pointer − a little device with wheels − that all the players put their hands on. A spirit will move the pointer and spell out words. You can ask questions and the spirit will answer you.'

'If you push the pointer, presumably.'

'Oh no. If everyone relaxes, just resting a finger on the pointer, it'll move by itself. It works just as well if you use an upturned glass.'

I must have looked dubious, because Mrs Dawson added, 'Try it, and you'll see.' Her voice then became confidential. 'Look. You don't want to stay messing around with services like this. Between you and me these open meetings are kid's stuff. Nothing important ever comes out. In my opinion their main function is to keep the older members happy. The spirits give out little cosy messages, but they don't really help you develop your psychic gifts.'

'There are far more effective means of contacting the other side than coming to church meetings. Ouija is one. Then, when you've cultivated your spiritual awareness, you can act as a medium − actually let the spirits use your body and speak through it. That's what really pleases them. These spirits haven't been in a human body, some of them, for centuries.'

'And what sort of spirits do you get?'

'All sorts. A lot of them are nobodies − I mean nobody important. But not all. I got King John the other day.'

'Do you ever get God?'

'Oh no. God doesn't speak, or get inside people. He is the principle of Total Love behind the universe. He will guide you, and I know one or two people who in a deep trance have actually seen him. But he's not a human spirit, you must remember that. The spirits who come at meetings like this have all at some time or other lived as men and women on the earth.'

'You must lead a dangerous life. What happens if you get Genghis Khan?'

But if Mrs Dawson saw the joke she chose to disregard it. 'No, it's quite wrong to think of evil as an absolute. All spirits are basically good, even the ones that were murderers and suchlike in their bodily form. They differ only in the degree of their love. God keeps them all in order, and anyway there's no danger if you drink some water afterwards. Water drives away any malign influence.'

She paused, and looked at me thoughtfully. 'Yes. I'm convinced you have the healing gift. You really must develop it.'

I shrugged. 'And suppose I do – what then?'

'Then you may become a very famous man, Mr Lee.'

Once again the remark struck home: it appealed to me very much to be famous. Immediately I suppressed the thought and made light of it.

'I'll believe that when it happens. Thanks – it's been good talking to you.'

I took my leave and rejoined Joanna who was standing near the door with her coat on. Most of the congregation had left.

'What did you find out?' she asked.

'Just about everything except the price,' I said with a smile. 'Mrs Dawson would be a bombshell in one of our showrooms. I'll ask her sometime whether she'd like to try her hand at selling electric cookers.'

'Do you think she was serious about the healing powers?'

'I'm sure she was. Salesmen are very serious people. They can talk the hind legs off a donkey if they smell a deal.'

'It doesn't sound like you're buying it.'

'No.' I took her arm and pushed open the door. 'So far the case is definitely unproven.'

But if the case was unproven it certainly wasn't closed. I made a conscious effort to ignore the message that had come to me. At the same time, I found myself driven to take the investigation further. I felt I simply had to get to the bottom of it and satisfy myself, one way or the other. The intensity of this urge surprised me, but I had no reason to question it.

In the course of the next week I tried several shops to get hold of a ouija board. None of them had one, and in the end I resorted to borrowing a book from the library and using its instructions to build my own. I cut out a large square of cardboard and wrote across the centre, in two slightly arching lines, the letters of the alphabet. In the top corners I put the words YES and NO respectively and, beneath the alphabet, the numbers one to nine, followed by a nought. At the very bottom I wrote GOODBYE in capitals. There were many intricate decorations on the plan I was using, mostly celestial figures like the sun and the moon, but I didn't feel it was worth reproducing these.

When I came to use the board I placed it in the centre of the dining-room table, and substituted for a pointer an ordinary drinking glass. I usually played with Joanna, and sometimes with the two elder children as well. The first few times the results were indifferent. Occasionally the glass seemed to move of its own volition, but most of the time I couldn't be sure if we were pushing it or not. I remained intensely interested, but unconvinced. Then, a few weeks after our visit to the spiritist church, something happened which changed the course of my life.

Joanna and I had cleared away the remains of dinner and I set out my improvised board on the table. We sat down. I folded back my notepad and laid it on the table in front of me. As usual we had a short silence before commencing, then rested our right-hand index fingers very lightly on the glass. Immediately I had the sensation that the board surface was as slippery as ice. When I asked, 'Is anyone there?' the glass slid smoothly and quickly to the YES.

Joanna and I exchanged glances. She had sensed it too.

'Who are you?' I said.

The glass moved rapidly to spell out M-O-T-H-E-R.

I thought a moment. 'When did you die?'

1-9-5-9.

'Ask her whose mother she was,' said Joanna.

'Whose mother are you?' I repeated, slowly and clearly.

Y-O-U-R-S.

'I looked up sharply at Joanna. 'You're pushing it.'

'I'm not.'

'You must be.'

But she replied vehemently, 'Robert, honest to God I am *not pushing it!*'

51

She was telling the truth. I looked at the glass, which was hovering above the letter S, and felt my stomach begin to turn. Messages from the other side were easy enough to handle when they were anonymous, but now that one claimed to come from my own mother I was losing my nerve. It was either some sort of horrible trick, or the medium had been right all along. There was only one way to find out.

'Spirit,' I said, 'what is your name?'

M-E-G.

I lifted my hand from the glass and slowly sat back in the chair. My parents had been dead now for months. There were probably less than half a dozen people alive who knew that my father had called his wife Meg. It was a pet name, one that he had used rarely if at all outside the privacy of their home. Her real name had been Maggie. Of course both Joanna and I knew the secret, but we knew also that the glass had moved quite independent of our own wills.

That left one possible explanation. That there was, in fact, a spirit world beyond our own where the ghosts of the dead were found, and that the spirit that had answered our summons tonight belonged to my mother. I looked across at Joanna and said, 'Case proven.'

We put the ouija board away. I felt an important milestone had been achieved and that it would in some way be inappropriate to carry on that evening. I felt also that I needed to think things over. Joanna went off into the front room where the children were watching television, and left me on my own.

For a long time I sat perfectly still with my arms folded on the table top. We hadn't drawn the curtains and where the windows looked out on the back garden I could see a dark reflection of the room. Nothing was very clear; we had played with the lights subdued, and Joanna hadn't turned them up on her way out. I appeared as a spectral figure hunched forward in thought. It seemed to fit my new situation very well.

The world was no longer the short-term affair I had thought it to be, in which a man struggled for a momentary success before death extinguished him for ever. Like everyone else, I would be living for a lot longer than I'd bargained for. This was reassuring; I'd never relished the prospect of rotting six feet underground. On the other hand it caused me a certain nervous apprehension, because I had no idea what lay on the 'other side' and would have liked to get a preview before I went.

But there were more urgent matters than that to consider right now. Evidently I was very gifted in spirit, and that would have important implications for the course of my present life. If Mrs Dawson was to be believed – and why now should she not? – I had in potential the ability to perform miraculous healings. A wild fantasy came to me: I saw myself walking through hospital wards, raising terminal cases from their beds while the doctors looked on in consternation. The media couldn't fail to take notice of that. Besides which, I would be doing a valuable service for mankind. I had always liked to think of myself as a philanthropist; and now, surely, the chance was being handed to me on a plate.

So far, however, it was only a chance. Gifts of healing needed to be cultivated, practised, learned, worked at. And Mrs Dawson hadn't offered to take me on as an apprentice; in fact she had spoken as if the art could be learned in total isolation. Her only advice was to approach the spirits – something that I had already begun to do. Yet the spirits were only dead people. Did they really know that much more about things like healing than men such as myself, who were still alive? Probably not. It followed then, that I should go straight to the top, and seek my instruction from God himself. According to Mrs Dawson, he wasn't above guiding people.

I pondered this for a while, then I got up and quietly closed the door, shutting out the noise of the television. For the first time in thirty years I was going to pray. My first inclination was to get down on my knees, but I stopped myself. God wasn't the sort of person Christians believed him to be. He didn't want people grovelling in front of him or pleading with him. It was far better to maintain my self-respect and present my requests in a cool, dignified way. I sat down again at the table, clasped my fingers and closed my eyes.

'God,' I said, 'I have now proven to my satisfaction that you actually exist. Having done this I now wish to serve you, and use my gifts in a way that will benefit mankind. I realise that I need your help in learning how to heal. It is my respectful request that you give me that help. I am willing to give you my time and my resources, within reason, and in exchange you will be the acknowledged power behind every healing that I perform.'

I wondered whether to add, 'Amen', but decided against it. That was too much like the prayers that orthodox, misguided people made, and probably wouldn't further my cause. Instead, I waited quietly. It was several moments later that I heard a voice speak, as clear as a bell in my mind.

It said, 'God is very pleased that you are seeking him. He has sent us to help you find your way.'

It was the Guide.

4: Descent into hell

I had been betrayed. I knew that now. The benevolent tones
employed by the Guide when I first met him made a stark
contrast with the voice I heard now – the Devil's voice, swearing
he would drive me insane. I glanced helplessly around the office,
trying to get a grasp on the everyday world and drag myself out
of this nightmare. But the room appeared dim and cavernous; it
was as if I'd been climbing down into hell and found the gate
closed behind me. Ahead the path plunged on downwards. I was
trapped.

In a way there was a kind of sick irony in it all. I had no doubt
that the voice belonged to the Devil – it was too starkly terrifying to come from anyone else. Yet I had been so cocksure that
the Devil didn't exist. It had been one of my first religious
decisions to consider him a figment of the imagination. Even
when, on entering spiritism, I acknowledged the existence of
God I gave not a moment's serious thought to the Devil. He had
stayed hidden until I was fully in the trap, and only now, when
I had no means of escape, had he dropped his disguise. For a
moment my mind skimmed back over the last few months in
sheer disbelief at my own blindness.

The voices had begun their work on a very low key. The first
part of my training (as they called it) consisted of a change in
diet. They told me I was eating far too much and that anyone
with hopes of becoming a healer should be a bit more frugal.
This was probably good advice. Business lunches were gener-
ous, not least because the girls in the canteen saw it as their duty
to fatten me up. I often arrived home to a cooked meal with no
appetite at all. So I took to eating smaller meals and sometimes

missed lunch altogether. As a result my infrequent visits to the canteen were greeted with good-natured cajolery. 'Hello! Where've you been, stranger?' the girls would say, and sometimes, 'Why, here's the walking rake!' It was true I was getting thinner. But I didn't mind them making fun of me because I felt a lot fitter.

During the course of the day one of the voices, usually the Guide, would talk to me. At first it happened seldom and irregularly. While I was mulling over the accounts one morning the Guide told me that my finance clerk, whom I had just seen, was having an affair with a secretary in the admin department. Allegations like this were never confirmed from other souces, but I took them as useful inside information. One couldn't tell when it might be necessary to apply pressure to a member of staff. In the end I built up quite an impressive dossier.

Very little of the training related to the art of being a healer. It was necessary first, the voices told me, to work on developing trust between myself and God. To this end they set me endless series of exercises, such as letting my mind go blank so that God could use it. They were particularly fond of talking to me at night. Few evenings went by without the Guide lecturing me or showing me bright animated pictures in the darkness. The time came when they were visible even in broad daylight, on a tall, door-shaped 'screen'. The pictures were meaningless: marching feet, moving lips, birds, clouds – but I followed them avidly, carried along on a tide of sheer enthusiasm.

It was only three or four months later that I started to flag. It wasn't that I lost any of my original zeal to obey God's instructions – I just felt the Guide was pushing me too hard. His interjections at work were happening now at more inconvenient times: when I was working to a deadline, or speaking at a conference. Often I barely stopped myself before answering back as if he were really in the room. All this was made worse by the fact that the evening lectures now went on into the early hours, causing me serious loss of sleep.

The first person I turned to was Joanna. As yet she knew nothing of the voices, and I had been thinking anyway that it was high time I shared my experiences with her. So one Saturday when the children were out I explained to her about the Guide and my secret training, and asked what people did when the spirits put them under too much pressure. But she brushed the question aside. This 'training', she said, accounted for my recent neglect of the family, and she was grateful after all this time to have received an explanation. It was long overdue. But so far as the voices were concerned, that was my own problem, and she could hardly be expected to sort it out. Why didn't I contact a medium?

Her reaction shocked me. It was quite true that my pursuits had taken me out of the house several nights a week, but it had never occurred to me that the family were suffering. I had always taken their love and support for granted. Now, apparently, I was neglecting them: I'd got two problems for the price of one. Still, I thought, there was nothing to be gained by worrying; I might as well take Joanna's advice and phone Mrs Dawson. At least if the first problem was sorted out there was a chance the second would simply disappear.

It took several attempts to find Mrs Dawson's number. There were scores of Dawsons in Watford and of course she was listed under her husband's initial. The phone rang for a long time before anyone picked it up.

'Hello?'

'Hello, I'm looking for Mrs Rose Dawson. Do I have the right number?'

'Mrs Dawson speaking.'

'Sorry to bother you, Mrs Dawson. This is Mr Lee.'

'Mr Lee?' she said, nonplussed.

'You met me a while ago at a spiritist church. I had the vibrations.'

She eventually caught on. 'Ah yes. Everything all right, I hope?'

'I'm not sure. I took your advice about the ouija board and I've become a fully committed spiritist. But I'm running into problems.'

'Oh?'

'I have voices that say God sent them to train me.'

'That's quite normal. They're familiar spirits. I have them, too.'

'But they won't leave me alone. Sometimes it's two in the morning before they let me go to sleep, and even then they wake me up in the middle of the night.'

'Have you spoken to them about it?'

'They say it's God's instructions. The training is too urgent to be stopped.'

There was silence on the end of the line. I said, 'Can't I see you and have you pray over me or something? It's not that I'm getting cold feet. I honestly want to be a healer. But I feel these familiar spirits might relax the pace a bit.'

'I'm not sure I could do that,' said Mrs Dawson, slowly. 'After all, God's instructions ought to be obeyed. I suggest if you're woken up you put on a light and read for a while. That'll soothe the mind, make it easier to drop off.'

'But I don't want to be woken up at all!'

'No, well, it's all part of the training, and it won't last for ever.'

'I hope not,' I said gloomily.

'Look on the bright side, Mr Lee. God wants you to be a big man. A man with strong healing powers, who can help people. It stands to reason that your training is rigorous.'

'Yes, of course, but ... ' I petered out. I wanted to say that the training had so far taught me nothing about healing and that in my weaker moments I wondered where it was all going to lead. But I knew that was being soft. I had to stick to my guns.

'No, you're right,' I said. 'I'm sorry if I sound like I'm complaining. I just felt I needed to compare notes. Would you mind if I phoned you from time to time for advice?'

'You'd do better to phone the Spiritist Centre at Amersham Place in Bristol. They'll give you more advice than I can. The number's in the book.'

I thanked her, and hung up.

The call had done me good. It was encouraging to talk to someone who believed in me and who knew the sort of trials I was going through. It had steeled my nerve. At the same time I felt slightly guilty at having needed to phone in the first place. For someone so greatly gifted in the healing vibrations I wasn't showing much stamina. In the Guide's words, God would not be pleased. I resolved to show my commitment by obeying his commands more ruthlessly than before. No one was going to call me a coward or a slacker.

But the pressure increased. One reason was that my life at home took a sharp turn for the worse. I could not make a show of enthusiasm for the training without keeping up my attendance at spiritist meetings. As a result I spent even ~~less~~ time with the family. This wouldn't have been so bad if I'd been a drinker, someone who habitually went out in the evenings, leaving the wife and children at home. But I had always been a family man; we took holidays and outings together, worked in the garden together, read together, ate together. When I went out my absence was keenly felt. Now that my activities used up four or five nights of the week there was a definite sense in the household that I was letting the side down. Joanna and the children started to carve out for themselves a life I took no part in.

On top of this I found the training steadily harder to cope with. The tasks set for me to do, to prove my trust in God, became progressively more bizarre. It was about this time that the visits began, of which the final one to *Gossander* was a typical example. Most of this I took in good humour, but fatigue occasionally made me short-tempered and I would ask the Guide what he thought he was doing. Complaints were angrily put down. I soon learned that if the voices couldn't get their way by persuasion they resorted to bullying.

I complied with their wishes as best I was able. Some of their commands were hair-raising. Once on the way back from work the Guide told me to relax my grip on the wheel and let *him* drive instead. I obeyed, and the car steered itself round four tight corners into the front drive.

At work the voices interfered almost continually. I couldn't do anything without having at the same time to carry on a conversation with the Guide or one of his friends. It was especially bad when I was in company. I found myself juggling with replies, some to my workmates, others, in my mind, to the spirits. I managed remarkably well, but the stress of sleepless nights was growing on me and it was only a matter of time before I got my wires crossed and answered the voices aloud.

It finally happened at a management consultation. These were held about once a month between the manager and his three immediate deputies, of whom I was one. Stan and I had been preparing for this particular meeting for weeks. We had some proposals to make which, if accepted, would alter the structure of the industry in our region. The manager had asked Stan for his plans on reshuffling the admin department. Stan was answering at some length, making gestures with his fountain pen and casting the occasional glance at me for support. All of a sudden the Guide said, 'You must get up, immediately.' I was trying hard to concentrate and before I could stop myself I said in a very irritable tone, 'Not now. I'm busy!'

Stan stopped dead. The manager looked at me and said, 'Pardon?'

I felt the blood rush to my cheeks. I coughed and mumbled that I had been thinking about something else and had inadvertently voiced my thoughts. They were very polite. The manager told Stan to continue and no more was said about the incident. That afternoon, however, Stan came into my office.

At first his manner was casual. We discussed how things had gone that morning and tried to assess the reaction of the meeting. In fact our proposals had been referred to a sub-committee, which might have been a covert way of shelving them. At any rate, it looked unlikely that any major changes would occur within the next six months. The topic was dropped. There was a short silence, then Stan said, 'You've had something on your mind lately, Bob.'

'Have I?'

'Come on, you don't need to kid me. A fellow doesn't yell out during a consultation when he's just daydreaming.'

'No, all right. I guess I've been under a bit of pressure with that development project. I worry about it more than I ought to.'

He pursed his lips. 'We all have problems like that.' There was a pause. 'Phyllis tells me you're interested in spiritism.'

'Spreading rumours about me again?' I joked.

'Hardly a rumour. You darn nearly dragged her into a seance, so I hear.'

'Yes, I admit I'm pretty enthusiastic about it. A sort of hobby. I go along to the spiritist church down the road, and play ouija in the evening. What's wrong with that?'

'Oh, I don't know,' said Stan. 'But it's always seemed a bit shady to me. The sort of thing you don't want to get too deeply involved in.'

'Oh, get off,' I chided him. 'It's no worse than gambling. And I know you have a little flutter on the horses from time to time.'

Stan smiled and stood up. 'I suppose not. By the way, how's that pretty wife of yours? I missed having the foxtrot with her at the last social.'

'She's fine. She just gets tired sometimes at the end of the week. Last Friday she let me go on my own.'

'Well, remember me to her. I'll see you around.'

He closed the door behind him, and I flopped back in my chair and groaned. There was no doubt that the boss had sent him in. It wasn't like Stan to pry. The tell-tale signs of stress were being picked up and investigated. Stan was a good friend and I hated having to stonewall him, but what else could I do? Had he been able to understand the pressure I was under I still couldn't have told him. If a whisper of my problem reached the manager's ears I'd find myself out in the dole queue. My only option was to keep on covering up. That wouldn't be easy – Stan had been perceptive enough to notice Joanna's absence from the last old-time dance – but there was no choice.

At the same time I knew I had to do something about the pressure of the training. Every time I raised the matter with the Guide he just laughed at me. It was lack of trust, he said. I gazed across the office, watching the sea of waving fists in the oblong screen. The voices babbled like a radio I could not turn off. It was a wonder that I could work at all under conditions like these. I pulled the Bristol telephone directory from its drawer and opened it on the desk in front of me. Sure enough, the Spiritist Centre was listed. But dare I phone? The voices could be nasty when they wanted to, and anyway they might be right in pointing out that weakness on my part would only prolong the training, not curtail it. I hesitated a long time before picking up the receiver.

They gave me an appointment for the following week. I awaited it apprehensively. I was acting against orders and expected at any moment that the blow would fall. But the Guide, though he must have known what I was doing, made no comment. That made me suspicious. It was possible that he misunderstood my motives, but I got the impression that he knew them only too well and was hanging back, waiting to see which way I would jump.

When the day came I was shown up to a studio room at the top of the Centre. I had been hoping for a frank talk with the office manager, but was told at reception that he was not available. The alternative was this one-hour session with a medium. I arrived to find all the blinds were down. The medium, evidently a famous one, gave me a brief handshake and introduced himself as Quentin Sykes. I expected him to ask me what I wanted, but he only led me to a plain, wooden chair and sat down opposite me in the semi-darkness. There was a pause. The medium had composed himself and was staring vacantly at my forehead.

'Can I tell you why I'm here?' I ventured.

Quentin Sykes didn't reply. He was in a trance.

'Can I tell you – ' I said again, but I couldn't rouse him. I sighed and waited to see what would happen.

After what seemed like an age a faint sound emerged from the medium's lips. At first just a mumble, it grew louder until words and sentences could be heard. I listened carefully. The speech, a continuous monologue, was rapid and confused. Phrases tumbled one into the next without any discernible order, and only occasional snatches made any sense. 'Chosen', he kept on saying, and 'Going to be a healer'. Then, 'Patience, be patient', and 'You must trust us'.

This was exactly the same sort of cacophony I had going on inside my own head. To hear it coming from Quentin Sykes, for whose services I was paying a great deal of money, was infuriating. 'Mr Sykes,' I said – but the words pouring out of his mouth drowned my own. They seemed to fill the great, attic room with whispers. 'Mr Sykes,' I repeated, loudly and firmly, 'I know all this already. You're just tuning in on the voices I hear all the time. What I want – ' I paused for breath. It was like battling against a sheer wall of sound. 'What I want is some advice on how to control them. Do you hear? Advice! I want some advice!'

The babbling subsided, and Mr Sykes came to. His eyes quivered slightly as if he were waking out of a deep sleep, then he stood up. He seemed almost surprised to see me.

'I do hope that was helpful to you,' he said, with a friendly gesture towards the door.

I felt like kicking him. I stood up abruptly and strode from the room. The session, I was sure, had been a calculated insult, a cruel joke stage-managed by the Guide. No wonder he had kept so quiet about my visit to the Centre. I stalked down the staircase, my footsteps echoing loudly. About half-way down I passed an exit on the second floor with a sign that said HEALING ROOM. I noted it as I went by, then stopped and, on an impulse, climbed back up the steps and walked in.

Inside it was much like a doctor's waiting-room, with chairs facing in towards a low coffee table on which lay a pot plant and a scatter of magazines – mostly spiritist periodicals. It was fairly crowded; in fact two of the occupants were leaning against the wall for lack of a seat. As I stood in the doorway a dapper young man in a black suit came in and said, 'Mrs Stanthorpe?' A woman in the corner packed her knitting away and started to get up. The young man, noticing me, said, 'It's a long wait, chum.'

'How long?'

'Couple of hours. We're behind, and one of the healers is away.'

He escorted the woman down a side passage and vanished from sight.

I made a snap decision to stay. Joanna would be expecting me for dinner, but I could phone and say I was going to be late. If these healers could help me it was worth hanging around. So I took my place by the wall and started thumbing through a magazine. The attendant put my name on the list when he returned. Three and a half hours later I was called.

The passage into which the other occupants of the waiting-room had one by one disappeared was short, with windows on one side and soiled grey doors on the other. I was shown through the second. The man sitting behind the desk was about twenty-five years old with thick spectacles that made his eyes look like fish. He was consulting his watch as I came in.

Last one,' said the attendant. The man at the desk looked noticeably relieved.

'Yes? he said as I sat down.

'I'm Mr Robert Lee.'

'Yes?'

'I have a problem with spirits.'

'Yes?' said the healer, a note of exasperation in his voice.

'They're pushing me around. They say God sent them to make me into a healer, but quite frankly they're getting to be a bit of a nuisance. I hardly get any sleep because they're talking to me, and I'm losing concentration at work.'

'Well, it's a fine time of night to get that one sorted out.'

'But can't you do something?'

He removed his spectacles, rubbed his eyes, and put the

spectacles back on again. 'Yes, I suppose we can do something. How long has this been going on?'

I told him. He then fired off a round of other questions which I had time to answer only in monosyllables.

'All right,' he said, finally, 'take your coat off and lie on the couch. I'm not promising any results, but I'll do what I can. That's it. Now lie still and look straight at the ceiling.'

He stood over me, his hands held palm downwards about six inches above my stomach. Slowly, I began to feel a warmth in my intestines.

'Anything happening?' he asked.

'I'm getting a slight burning sensation.'

The healer withdrew his hands, clapped them together, kneaded them, and put them back. The warmth returned, more intense this time. 'Any change?'

'Yes. It's hotter; quite painful.'

'Fine. Just hold it. The heat is a sign of the healing vibrations. It won't do you any harm.'

I was biting my lip by this stage. Still, he seemed to be on the right track because the voices, usually muttering loudly in my head, were dying down a bit. I envied him the ability to control them and reflected that I had a lot to learn before I became a healer. I listened as he repeated prayers under his breath and wondered how long it would be before I could do the same thing. Paradoxically, I had come to resent the training, yet I wanted also to go through with it. The same stubborn streak in my nature that rebelled at the bullying of the Guide also kept me resolute in my determination to become a healer.

The voices faded to a murmur. The heat was getting very painful, and I thought I was going to have to ask the healer to stop when suddenly he withdrew his hands and the burning ceased. It was as if a red-hot branding iron had been lifted off my skin. I sat up, a little giddy.

'That should do it,' said the healer. He was plucking his overcoat from a peg on the back of the door. 'Try and take things easy; a couple of days off work, maybe. Soon you'll be back to normal. Here — your jacket.'

I took it. 'I can still hear the voices, though,' I said.

'You'll find them far more subdued from now on.'

'But can you tell me what's been happening to me, and what

I can do if the training goes wrong again?'

'Look, I'm sorry, Mr Lee,' he said, reaching for the light switch, 'I have an urgent appointment and I can't stay to answer any questions. Believe me, you've been healed and you'll have no more trouble. Now, if you would be kind enough to take this bill to the desk downstairs they will tell you how much to pay. Excuse me.'

I paid and took the next train home. It was past nine. The call-box in the Spiritist Centre was out of order so Joanna would have no idea where I was. I flopped into a seat on the train and gazed at my reflection in the window. The train roared from one station to the next. All the stops looked the same: tiled walls, advertisements, dingy old men nodding on the benches. Other passengers came and went with their books and bags and newspapers. I didn't take much notice of them. It was eight stops along the line that the Guide spoke to me.

I had almost expected it. The last few hours, the last week's furtive preparation, now seemed a completely futile exercise. The Guide had known all along. He had watched me running, and now that I had worn myself out he was pulling me in on a rope. The healer had done nothing permanent to ease my condition. He had given me a dose of morphine that would soon wear off. He and Quentin Sykes had probably been in on the conspiracy from the start.

'Why did you go to the healer?' said the Guide.

'I don't know,' I said. It was safe to speak aloud; the noise of the train obliterated the words as soon as they left my mouth.

'Are you dissatisfied with your training?'

'I don't know.'

'Perhaps you hoped to get rid of me?'

The tone was menacing. I squirmed. 'I don't know.'

I really didn't know. I felt I didn't know anything any more. Yes, I wanted to be a healer, and yes, I was finding the training too much, and yes, I wished the voices would go away, and yes, I was determined to go through with it all to the bitter end. I was confused and too tired to start sorting things out. Until I knew what to say, I wished the Guide would leave me alone. I maintained a dejected silence.

'The training can't be stopped, Robert.' The voice was thick and harsh. 'Now that you've begun you've got to go on with it.

65

Running away won't make it finish any quicker, so don't try any more tricks like you did today. God's not fooled.'

'No,' I said, miserably. 'No, I'm sorry.'

'And you'll be more sorry.'

A numbness came over my face, as if an ice-cold hand had been placed over it. I felt the cheek muscles distend and the eyes narrow. They were beyond my control. I tried to stop them but my nerves were paralysed. For a moment I thought my face was going to be ripped in two, then the rebellious muscles froze. When I looked at my reflection I could barely recognise myself. My features had been taken over by a broad, sly, oriental smile. Everyone else in the carriage was staring at me. I looked like a statue of the Buddha.

That expression returned to my face whenever the Guide wanted to assert his authority over me. He had little enough reason to do it. From that evening any illusion of independence on my part was unequivocally shattered. My training allowed me no more freedom than that of the newest recruit in the forces. My spiritual masters drove me on without mercy. If before they had been bullies, now they were tyrants.

The training went on at an accelerated pace. There were more petty tasks, more lectures, more visits, more absurd images looming in my inner vision. If I obeyed I received lavish praise and assurances that the training would soon be over; if I was stubborn, or failed at a task, I was scolded or punished. The training dominated my waking hours. In fact I was lucky if I escaped it for more than a brief spell by sleeping at night. Relationships in the normal world were maintained only by a tremendous effort of will. In my home they were hardly maintained at all. I generally returned late in the evening to find my dinner cooked dry in the oven, and rose in the morning to eat breakfast alone. Joanna, probably wisely, kept the children out of my way, and restricted her own conversation with me to the barest essentials. If we discussed my problem at all it was only to ask me why I was being such a fool. I answered evasively. I tried to assure her that things would soon be back to normal. But I felt wretched; the matter had really passed beyond my control.

Two things kept me sane. One was the assurance, given frequently by the Guide, that God was pleased at my efforts to serve him. Through all my suffering I clung to the hope that one day I would pass the test and qualify to be a healer. It might be trial by fire, but there was an end to it. The other thing was the provision of sleeping pills. I went to the local doctor and told him I was in a fix and needed something to help me sleep. I managed to sidestep his questions. The small green and white capsules he gave me became my lifeline to rest. Because my thoughts had become almost continually depressing I would lie in bed with a pile of comic books, take two or three capsules, and read myself to sleep. That way at least I kept the voices at bay for a while.

But in the end came the experience that convinced me, finally, that I was about to crack. It was long past midnight. Joanna was already asleep when I arrived home. I undressed and fell into bed, exhausted but wakeful, ready to read pages of strip cartoons until I dozed off. I swallowed a couple of pills and began reading. They seemed to work quite fast. When I felt drowsy enough to sleep I switched off the light. But no sooner was I lying down than the voice of the Guide forced its way into my mind.

'Wake up!' he said. 'God wants some work done on you.'

This was new. 'What sort of work?' I asked, barely conscious.

'To make you into a healer. It's necessary for the structure of your brain to be changed.'

'Changed? How?'

'We're going to insert a steel pin through your skull.'

I was fully awake now. I realised with horror that the Guide didn't joke about things like this. They were really going to do it. I jerked up, but immediately a pair of invisible fists grasped my shoulders and forced me down on to my back. 'No!' I yelled, almost hysterical, 'No! I don't want it!'

I was squirming, tossing my head from side to side, screaming to be spared. But the spirits took no notice, and Joanna, though I must have been raising the roof, slept on soundly. Gradually the fists immobilised my body until I lay rigid, sweating with terror. I could hear the Guide supervising the operation. It was like being tied, blindfold, to a stake, hearing the order given, the faint brush of the rifle butts against the uniform, the click of the cocks, trying to judge when the handerchief would fall.

When, a few days later, the God I had followed so faithfully told me he was going to drive me mad, I knew he meant it. The pain was so indescribable that just thinking of it in my office on that Tuesday afternoon brought on a wave of nausea. There was no way I could survive another night like that. I had only got through the last one because I had passed out. If the same thing happened again — and surely this time round it would be infinitely worse — then there were only two possibilities. Either I would wake up insane, or I wouldn't wake up at all.

It was a grim choice! But at least now all the cards were on the table. I knew what I had long suspected but never dared admit to myself — that the training was a decoy. I probably had no gift of healing; I just liked to think I had, and that had been used to lure me into the trap. But what sort of trap was it? I tried to think calmly and clearly. It wasn't easy; I could feel a wild thudding inside my chest: if I wasn't careful I was going to have a coronary to add to my list of problems. *Trap*, I thought, marshalling my thoughts with an effort, *a trap set by the Devil*. But what interest did the Devil have in me? Who *was* the Devil, anyway?

Suddenly, out of the fog that seemed to surround me, came the two iron fists. I was crushed forwards over the desk. I could see the outline of the room only dimly now. The rest of the building might have been in another universe. Inch by inch the fists drove my head down on to the blotting pad. I soon felt its rough surface wedged against my face; I was being squashed against it like plasticine. Painfully, I levered myself upright; then, out of the fog, I saw the door swing open and recognised Stan's face looking in.

'Crikey!' I heard him say. 'You all right, Bob?'

'Yes! Yes!' I shouted back perversely. 'Yes, I'm all right.'

He didn't seem to be moving.

'Leave me! I'm all right, I said.'

The door closed, or the fog enveloped it, I don't know which. 'Well, that's it,' I said to myself, bitterly. 'All the chickens are coming home to roost. The manager's going to be in here in a minute and I'll lose my job before I lose my sanity.'

I sat there, humiliated, helpless, and able only to think what a complete idiot I'd been for the last forty years. It all came back to me. The day I listened to Mr Hartley and decided the Devil didn't exist; the scorn I had poured out consistently on the Christian Church as being a group of hypocritical, misguided do-gooders; my investigation of spiritism that I had considered so grand and scientific; and finally, the conceited and frankly ridiculous notion that I was going to be a world-famous healer.

What a dupe I had been! Of course I could lay the blame on a score of other people for leading me astray, but in the end a man was responsible for his own actions, and I had of my own choice walked straight into hell. The irony of it! Two years ago I'd have laughed if I'd seen someone in my position now. I'd have said he was mentally ill. It would never have crossed my mind that he was at the mercy of the Devil.

Self-reproach burned away and left a small residue of despair. After all, it mattered very little now whose fault it was. I might as well face up to it and shoulder the blame. I was only sorry that so many other people had suffered through my ignorance. In particular I was sorry for my family. I had not only made Joanna and the children join me in my spiritist pursuits but I had ruined our home into the bargain. Perhaps I would have the chance to make it up to them? I doubted it. The Devil had been playing with me for a long time and now that I was safely in his net I would be very swiftly disposed of. Nobody pushed the Devil around.

A huge emptiness seemed about to engulf me. My mind was teetering on its brink, repeating aimlessly the words, *Nobody pushes the Devil around, nobody pushes the Devil around*. Over and over it went, like a scratched gramophone record. With every repetition it became more devastating and final. I knew for certain that I was on the way out. Eight, maybe ten hours remained to me of life as I had known it, and then, tonight, the Devil would return and keep his promise. He would drive me insane.

And the story might have ended there. But at that moment, from I don't know what recesses of my memory, there welled up into my mind a name I hadn't thought of for years.

Jesus.

5: On the run

Jesus Christ was to the best of my knowledge the one person who *had* pushed the Devil around, and done it with impunity.

In my state of semi-stupor the memory returned with startling vividness. I saw Mr Hartley reading out the passage on the temptation from the Gospel of Matthew. He was walking up and down, stooped in that characteristic way he had, holding the book a few inches from his nose. He had read out the three temptations, including the one where the Devil asks Christ to worship him, and had reached the last of Christ's replies:

'Get thee hence, Satan: for it is written, Thou shalt worship the Lord thy God, and him only shalt thou serve.'

At that point Mr Hartley had looked up and, removing his spectacles, said with an air of finality, 'And the Devil departed.' What Mr Hartley had gone on to say in his conversation with me had been totally misleading, but these words, read straight from the Gospel, came through now with the force of a bullet. Blindly, instinctively, I heaved in a breath. 'Jesus! Jesus!' I cried. 'Jesus, help me!' My tongue was as dry as a bone and I started to cough, but I kept on calling out, my whole energy bent to the task. 'Jesus! Save me! Jesus!'

The effect was dramatic. Immediately, the invisible iron fists were lifted, and I slumped backwards into the chair. Everything seemed to be tilting sideways. I struggled to keep a grip on my senses, still gasping out the name with every breath. Gradually the room was losing its subterranean atmosphere; the fog was clearing and through the windows I could see the grey belly of the clouds. Natural daylight once again flooded the room.

Out of the confusion I heard the voice of the Guide. 'Stop that!' he was saying. 'Don't be a fool! There's nothing you can do.'

But I was beyond listening to him. I went on crying out, almost in tears, 'Jesus, I know you're more powerful than the Devil. He couldn't tempt you. You told him to go away, and he had to go. I'm sorry I haven't believed in you. Help me. Please!'

'No one can help you now,' snapped the Guide. 'Stop squealing!'

'Jesus can help me. I know he can. He must,' I sobbed.

'Jesus hated scum like you.'

I covered my head with my hands, shaking convulsively. 'Jesus ... Jesus!'

'And where is he, this Jesus?' the Guide asked, sarcastically.

'I don't know. But he's somewhere. And he'll help me, I know he will.'

'If you can find him,' jeered the Guide. 'How do you know he's still alive? We crucified him, remember.'

I grasped the edge of the desk and pulled myself up. 'I'll find him. Just you see.' For a moment I stood, swaying slightly, letting my mind clear. Everything looked abnormally bright and clear. My mind took in specks of dirt on the windows and the small dents in the partition where people leaned into it on their way out of the room. Jesus must be somewhere, as real as those details of my office. Swallowing hard, I made for the door, opened it, and went out.

I walked hurriedly along the corridor, past Stan's office and the typing pool and round the corner. Ignoring the lift, I pushed through a fire-door and clattered down the stairs. At the bottom I caught Fred, bent over a crossword. He stood up with a jerk and made to swing open the door, but I was through it already and running across the car park.

'You're crazy,' said the voices. 'Go back to your office. If anyone finds out what you're doing you'll get fired.'

I refused to pay attention. As soon as I could wrestle my key into the ignition I was off, doing a sharp reverse turn then jamming the gears into first to take the gates. Two pedestrians dodged aside. I reached a noisy halt at the junction, then, barely glancing to check if I was clear, swerved out on the open road. I was taking the route to Ilford, but I had no intention of stopping there. I was on my way to Central London.

If I was going to find Jesus anywhere I reckoned I would find him in a church; and there was only one church I had ever taken much notice of – the Catholic church on Kingsway. I'd looked in there years ago, just to sneer, and walked in on the afternoon Mass. If that service was still being held the chances were that someone there would be able to help me find Jesus.

'You expect the Catholics to help you?' I heard the Guide say. 'They're hypocrites. You know that.'

'Not all of them' I breathed. 'They can't be. Some of them must be sincere.'

'And what if they are? Why should they do anything to help you? You haven't exactly done them any favours lately.'

'It doesn't matter. They're kind people.'

'They stink. You said so yourself.'

'I know I did and I'm sorry I was such a fool. I'm going to apologise to them.'

'They'll kick you out as soon as look at you.'

I gripped the wheel tightly. 'I'm going. You can't stop me.'

The voices snarled, but they didn't strike back. 'Go then! But don't expect them to save you. You're finished.'

'Jesus,' I prayed under my breath, 'Jesus, please help me.'

There was a raucous laugh. The image of a crucifix flew into my mind, and seemed to hover on the road ahead of me. 'That's the Jesus the Catholics worship. He's just a dead body,' the voices said. 'Why pray to a dead body? Do you think a corpse is going to save you from us? He couldn't even save himself. He talked a lot about saving others and did a few simple miracles, but we got him in the end. He couldn't stand up to the Devil.'

For an instant my foot slackened on the accelerator, but I pressed it down again. Jesus *had* stood up to the Devil, I knew that much. I forced the picture of the crucifix out of my mind and tried to remember what the Gospels said about him. It was a long time since I'd read them – way back before my confirmation, in fact. Only a few disjointed images returned: Jesus driving the money-changers from the temple with a whip; blind men and lepers; a crowd of thousands fed from a single basket of bread. I sifted through them in an attempt to make sense of my half-forgotten childhood beliefs. Never in my adult life had I thought those memories so precious.

For months it had all been so simple. There was a supernatural world presided over by God and peopled by the spirits of the dead. You could talk to them and learn from them, but there was no antagonism and certainly no such thing as evil. Everything ran on the principle of Total Love. Now I suddenly found myself faced with the Devil, as stark an opponent to Total Love as I could hope to find. Lined up behind him were a host of dark spirits, not the innocuous dead people Mrs Dawson had talked about, but positively evil creatures in the Devil's pay.

I felt like a prisoner on the run from Colditz. It was hard to believe that there were places still free from enemy control, so strong was his presence around me. And even if I managed to reach them, would I be recognised or accepted? In one way the Guide was right. Up to the present I had lived a totally irreligious life, and not just in the intellectual sense, either. Behind my respectable, middle-class exterior I was pretty corrupt, fiddling my expense account and keeping a box full of soft porn magazines to browse through in the loft. All that would recommend me well enough to the God I had been serving, the God who was in fact the Devil; but what about the *real* God?

That God and the Jesus of my childhood seemed very remote. For a start I could hardly remember anything about them. But the gap was not simply one of time. I felt now that, although I hadn't known what I was doing, in committing myself to the Guide and his master the Devil, I had absorbed something of their nature. In an unfathomable way I *belonged* to them. As soon as I thought that, I knew I was right. A phrase emerged with crystal clarity from the mists of my early, lost belief – *possessed of evil spirits.* I couldn't tell where it came from; it brought to mind only some dim, shadowy figure encountered by Jesus in the Gospels. But I knew for a fact that it applied also to me. I was possessed! A chill came over me. The Guide and the other voices were evil spirits living like parasites in my being. True, they were under a temporary restraint, but that wouldn't last for ever. I sensed instinctively that if I didn't somehow find this Jesus before nightfall, I was done for.

The mid-afternoon traffic was light and I made quick progress. Swinging round into Kingsway I glimpsed the Catholic church to my left. I prayed that it would be open. Kingsway was a broad street with taxi ranks in the centre but little parking space at the kerbs. I crawled up one way looking for a slot, found nothing, did a sharp U-turn and raced back. There was no point in wasting time. When I neared the church again I braked clumsily in the middle of the street and jumped out.

There was a blaring of horns. A taxi skidded to a stop in front of me, and the driver leaned from his cab to yell at me as I dashed to the pavement. I reached the double doors of the church in a few seconds, fought with them, and pushed my way through to the porch. Here I paused, glancing ahead of me into the church.

Beyond the glass inner doors the main aisle led up to an altar. Above that, mounted on a tall freestanding arch and lit dimly by the tiny latticed windows in the roof, I could see a crucifix. Over to the right a shorter, second aisle terminated in another altar, heavily decorated with flowers and painted gold. Between the two was a life-sized plaster facsimile of Christ.

Sure enough, there was a service going on. The pews were dotted with worshippers, on their knees with books open in front of them. On the steps before the altar a priest in white robes stood with his back to the congregation, arms raised in the air. I looked from the priest to the statue of Jesus and back again. I had no experience of Catholic churches. But the urgency of my situation forbade me to stand around watching, doing nothing, so I went in and hurried to the altar rail.

The priest was praying, his back still turned.

I leaned over the rail and called in a hoarse whisper, 'Father! Father!'

The priest took no notice.

I tried again. 'Father! I need some help.'

This time he faltered momentarily and glanced over his shoulder. I thought for a moment that he might come down and talk to me, but instead he just turned back and resumed the Mass. I spoke a third time, louder and more urgent than before. 'Please, Father, I'm possessed of evil spirits. You've got to pray for me.'

It was no use. He seemed determined to ignore me. I stood back, feeling slightly embarrassed. It was clear that I was causing a disturbance; some of the congregation behind me were looking up, waiting to see what I would do. I cast another glance at the priest. I seemed to remember that the altar was considered very holy by the Catholics. Was that where I would find Jesus? I contemplated jumping the rail and approaching it. But what then?

'If you want help,' whispered a man behind me, 'the place to go to is the confessional.'

He pointed across the other aisle at three confession boxes tucked away beneath the arches. Each one had a pair of plain wooden doors and a queue of people standing outside. I remembered seeing them in films.

I followed his direction to join one of the queues, passing as I did so the plaster effigy of Christ. The faded white face gazed calmly ahead, oblivious of priest and penitent alike, aloof from the cares and troubles of the world. I let my hand brush against it as I went by. It was cold.

It took about fifteen minutes to get into the confessional. There were two women ahead of me, shoppers by the look of them, and an old man with flu who kept on sneezing and pinching his nose. The first woman sat with a scarf on her head, bowed in prayer. The others looked this way and that, much as if they were lining up outside a public telephone. From behind me came the sound of light, tinkling bells and the smell of incense. I shuffled and fretted, folding my arms and consulting my watch. At last the old man emerged and knelt down before the golden altar. I went in.

Though the cubicle had an open roof it was very gloomy. It contained a chair, which faced the door, and in the place where a window might have been there was an iron grille. I caught a brief glimpse of the priest as I sat down. I said, almost immediately, 'Look, I'm sorry about creating a disturbance out there. I really didn't know what to do.'

He made no reply. I went on, 'In fact I'm sorry about a lot of things. For one, I've spent most of my life as an atheist, and I admit I've said some pretty awful things about religion and religious people. Especially, if you'll forgive me, Father, about Catholics. I've always said you're a lot of hypocrites and good-for-nothings and — well — I shouldn't go into details. But I'm sorry and I want to take it back. Will you listen to me?'

'Go on,' he replied, quietly.

I felt I wanted to tell him everything, it was such a relief to have a sympathetic ear. 'You see,' I said. 'I'm in a lot of trouble, Father. I left the Church, thinking that religion was a waste of time, and then, last year, I started going to the spiritists. I wanted to prove if the afterlife was real or not. Well, it is. I know it is, now. But I've got trapped by it. There's voices in my head that tell me what to do. And I've just found out they're spirits serving the Devil. Father, I'm possessed of evil spirits!'

The priest cleared his throat.

'I came here — in spite of all I've said about you — because you believe in Jesus. I know he's more powerful than the Devil. I want to believe in him, but I don't know how. Can you help me? I'm desperate, Father. If I don't get help before tonight I'm going to be driven mad.'

I waited for him to reply, and a long silence set in. At first I thought he was considering what I'd said, or praying over it, or composing a response. But the silence went on. Suddenly a fear seized me that I had been misunderstood. Perhaps he wasn't taking me seriously, or suspected me of playing a practical joke. 'Father!' I whispered, imploringly, 'I mean it. I need help.'

At length he said, 'Come round to the vestry at seven o'clock tonight. We'll see if anything can be done.'

Something in his tone of voice told me that he didn't hold out much hope. 'Can't you pray for me now, Father?' I said.

He didn't reply.

'I only want to find Jesus, that's all.'

Still there came no answer. I started to raise my voice. 'For crying out loud, you must be able to help me! I'm possessed. Can't you do anything?'

But nothing I said would coax another word out of him. This coyness baffled me. It wasn't as if there were another thirty people waiting to make their confessions when I left: I was the last in the line. He could easily be praying for me if he wanted to. Nor could the case before him have been more in need of attention. Among all the problems churchmen had to deal with it was hard to imagine a worse one than possession by evil spirits.

Suddenly I realised what was happening. This priest didn't believe a word I'd said. All my talk about the Devil and the voices was being taken as evidence of a mental disorder. In his opinion I needed not prayer but a psychiatrist. This stirred me so deeply that I was on the point of arguing with him, but stopped myself, knowing there was nothing to be gained by it. It is a sure sign of mental instability when the victim asserts that he is completely sane! The confessional seemed to close round me like a coffin. The voices had got me, after all. I'd raced all the way down here only to find that no one took me seriously. I raised both fists in a gesture of angry despair, and got up.

The plaster Christ watched serenely as I trudged out towards the porch. Nobody followed me or asked me what was the matter. For all it meant to me they might have been made of plaster and fixed permanently in their pews. I left feeling sick at heart. For the first time since the invisible fists had been prised off me in the office I was on the point of giving up. Jesus seemed so remote, so unreal. The clamour of voices was back again, and I was beginning to see the old familiar images flitting around on the fringes of my vision.

I had one more idea to try. If the Catholics couldn't tell me anything about Jesus then perhaps the Protestants could. I was a member of the Church of England, even if I'd never been near a church since my confirmation. At least they wouldn't turn me out. I crossed Kingsway and walked up a little way on the other side. The sky was very overcast now and it was starting to spit; the pavement in front of me was freckled with raindrops. I turned up the collar of my jacket and proceeded, clasping my lapels together with one hand. I hadn't been walking for three minutes when I came across Holy Trinity. It was set back from the street, with a broad terrace leading up to the doors. Carved in large letters above the entrance were the words, ENTER, REST AND PRAY.

A wave of relief came over me. Here at last was a church that made an open invitation to strangers to come and find help. There would surely be a minister here to speak to me. I ran up the steps on to the terrace and grasped the great black handles of the door.

It was locked.

I hammered at it and shook it. But the door didn't budge an inch, and nobody came to open it. I searched for another way in. To either side of the main entrance were small gateways, leading on one side to a fire escape and on the other to a slim courtyard. I tried these, too. Both were fastened with heavy padlocks. Even the notice-board gave only the name of the minister, his qualifications, and the time of the next Sunday's service. Nothing about Jesus. Nothing of the slightest use to a man possessed by evil spirits who knew next Sunday would be too late.

I stood back for a moment looking up at the inscription, the rain thudding heavily on my shoulders. The words were as useless to me as a menu outside a restaurant is to a man with no money. I felt like a tramp staring in as the head chef dresses a leg of mutton, hungry but condemned for ever to watch other people eating. Perhaps the voices had been right after all. Perhaps Jesus didn't go for people with a record like mine, and I was just kidding myself that I was going to escape. It was like the Guide to let me run free for a while so they could enjoy the chase before pulling me back in for the kill. Sooner or later I'd have to drive back home, chided and chastised as I had been on my return from the Spiritist Centre. At least then I still had hope.

Turning, I stumbled back across Kingsway. The rush hour was beginning now. The street was thick with buses and taxis, glossy in the rain, crammed full of city workers on their way home to a hot meal and an evening's easy viewing in front of the television. The *Aldwych, Victoria* and *Earl's Court* buses drove past me, windscreen wipers thudding back and forth. I joined the throng on the pavement and was carried along towards Holborn Underground. The surge of activity was overpowering. Men and women pushed and jostled each other in their hurry to reach the station. Every one of them had somewhere to go and something to do. Among them I was like a snared log on a river.

The sheer, oppressive reality of it all made me balk. Cars and pedestrians, lamps and illuminated signs, the wind and the rain and the ceaseless motion. These things crowded through my senses and left me in no doubt that they were real, that they existed. Of course I needed none of them. I wouldn't have been sorry if I'd never seen a car again my whole life long. But Jesus — Jesus who I needed and wanted more than anything else — was nowhere to be found. Was he dead? It seemed as if my chase had led me up a blind alley.

Alone on the crowded street I leaned my forehead against a lamp post and closed my eyes.

6: The long night

'Wizard. Absolutely Wizard.'

'Is he really?'

'No one like him. I last heard him speak in Margate. Held his audience spellbound.'

Two men appeared to have stopped on the street corner behind me. Their loud, enthusiastic conversation jarred my nerves, but I didn't bother to move, or even to open my eyes. The first, who had a higher, more cultivated voice than the other, said, 'He's written books, apparently. Wish I could get hold of one.'

'There's a good second-hand place near me,' said the other. 'What are the titles?'

A bus rounded the bend and drowned most of the reply. I heard, 'absolute best is ... I forget the name, but it's a first-rate treatment of Jesus' parables of the kingdom. Morrison's read it. Said if you're trying to get into the thought of the Synoptic Gospels nothing could be – '

He stopped as I turned round. 'Are you ministers?' I said.

'Yes.' The word was pronounced as a question. The first speaker, a lean young man with a rosy complexion and a prominent Adam's apple, was looking at me as if I were about to pull a revolver on him.

'You know about Jesus?'

'Well, yes ... ' The two men glanced at one another.

I lurched forward and grasped the taller one by the lapels. 'Please, you've got to help me!' He took a step backwards then stood his ground. His friend came between us and forced us apart, and we stood confronting each other in the rain.

'Really, have a care!' said the first, straightening his coat. The other, a stouter and slightly older man with black, curly hair, took me by the arm and looked me full in the face. 'Now, what's up?' he said gently.

'I'm possessed,' I muttered, hardly daring to look at him.

'Possessed?'

'Of evil spirits. Like it says in the Gospels you were just talking about. The Devil sent them and they say they're going to drive me mad. That's why I want Jesus ... '

I petered out into silence. I fully expected them to laugh in my face or tell me I needed a psychiatrist. But the curly-haired man only said, 'Let's get out of the rain. We can't talk properly out here. Phil, pick up my umbrella, will you?'

We retreated into the station entrance and found a corner where we were out of the crowd.

'Now, tell us what's been going on,' the shorter man said.

I explained, in a very garbled way, how I'd got interested in spiritism and started hearing the voices, and how the training they'd given me was making a wreck of my life and my marriage. The two men listened gravely and did not interrupt. I finished by telling them about the events of that morning and what had happened in the Catholic church.

'I think the priest was going to send me away for medical treatment,' I said. 'Is that what you'd do?'

'No,' said the curly-haired man. 'I believe you when you say you're possessed.'

'Can you do anything?'

He frowned slightly. 'We'll certainly try. I and my friend here have never had to handle a case like yours. But we're attending a conference at the City Temple and there are several more experienced men there we can refer you to.' He turned to his friend. 'Look, Phil, I think we should phone through and make arrangements, then we can take this fellow along with us for the evening session. Would you hang on here and look after him?'

Phil consented and we stood together as the other man wound his way through the crowds to a row of brown telephone boxes on the far side.

'Are you Church of England?' I asked, timidly.

'No, Presbyterian,' said Phil with a nervous, condescending smile. 'But don't worry. Presbyterians believe in Jesus.'

I'd never heard of Presbyterians before. The name sounded

fairly imposing, and I reassured myself that I was in safe hands. The conversation lapsed between us until the curly-haired man came back.

'All fixed up,' he said. 'I'm afraid the minister I've spoken to won't be free to see you until after the session, but you can come along and sit in the lobby till it's over. Now, we'd better get moving. Are you on foot?'

'No, my car's just round the corner.'

We went back out in the rain and found the Consul parked exactly where I'd left it in the middle of Kingsway. It was causing something of a traffic jam. We got in and drove the mile or so to the City Temple. There were no parking spaces here, either, so after trying a couple of streets I nudged the car into the kerb on Holborn Circus.

We got to the City Temple about fifteen minutes before the session was due to begin. A few late arrivals were still coming in, but most people must have already been there because a loud buzz of conversation could be heard from the main hall. A woman with a green badge was standing at the door, greeting everyone and handing out hymn-sheets. The curly-haired minister took me over to her.

'This is Dolly Cleeson, a member of my congregation.'

I introduced myself. Dolly Cleeson, a woman with an ambitious perm and a warm, indulgent smile, held out her hand. 'Pleased to meet you.'

'Dolly, would you mind looking after Mr Lee while I go in? He's here to see Don Carroll, but he's got to wait till after the meeting.' She nodded, and the minister turned to me. 'Now, you said you have a wife and family, Mr Lee. Are they expecting you to be out late?'

'No, but it's not unusual nowadays.'

'Then I think you ought to phone them. It's the right thing to do. Dolly will show you to the call-box. Please excuse me – I may see you afterwards.'

He disappeared through the doors and into the main hall. I could hear an amplified voice praying, then announcing a hymn. There was a rustling sound as people rose to their feet; the organ started up, and they began singing. The tune was vaguely familiar. Dolly closed the doors softly and led me down to where a public telephone hung on the wall. I didn't see much point in phoning, but I did as I was asked.

Joanna answered. 'Hello?'

'Hello, darling. I wanted to let you know I'll be late tonight, so you needn't wait up.'

'You don't usually bother to call.'

'No, well, I thought I should.'

'Suit yourself. Shall I keep your dinner or throw it out?'

'Er − oh, do as you like; I don't care. Actually I'm up at the City Temple with the Presbyterians.'

'Well, that's your business.'

'They said they might be able to help me.'

'I hope they do.' She said it entirely without emotion.

'I'll see you tomorrow, then,' I said.

'All right.'

'Goodbye, darling.'

She hung up. It was as I expected. My whereabouts was a matter of indifference to her; the City Temple or the Spiritist Centre or some obscure seance, it didn't matter which. For her it was another evening spent looking after the children on her own. And she knew that the next morning I would be drifting around, insisting that everything was OK, and looking like death itself. I really couldn't blame her for being so offhand.

The receiver was humming. I put it back and returned to the lobby, where Dolly was chatting to another usher. I hadn't seen him before. He had evidently been showing people to their seats and now that the conference was under way he had come out to stand at the doors. He was a lanky fellow with lurid socks and Buddy Holly glasses. He smiled as I came in; Dolly turned round.

'Oh, how did you get along?'

'Fine.'

She introduced her friend as Jim Harris. 'Call him Jim,' she added, convivially. 'You don't mind, do you, Jim?'

'Robert,' I said, trying to match the favour.

'Have you come for the conference?' Jim asked.

'No, he hasn't,' Dolly put in abruptly. 'He's here to see the Rev Carroll. He's just waiting till after the meeting.'

I nodded weakly.

'Of course you can always go in and sit at the back if you want,' she said to me, as an afterthought.

Part of me wanted to go right up on the platform and ask for help. But that was absurd. I replied simply, 'No thank you, I'd rather not.'

In fact I was starting to feel rather sick. The voices had come back strongly. They made a clamour in my head like a full-scale cavalry charge, with groans and shouts that I could not interpret. Superimposed on the ushers I was seeing a twisted, grey tree growing up out of the marble floor. It reached its branches into the air as if seeking something to clasp hold of, then shrivelled and faded.

'Can I sit down anywhere?' I said.

Dolly rushed to find me a chair. 'Of course. You're not looking well, are you? Poor thing.'

I sat down heavily.

'Goodness, he is looking pale, Jim. We ought to get him something. Robert, would you like some tea?'

I made a faint sign of assent, and Jim was dispatched to get it. 'See if there's any biscuits, too,' Dolly called after him. 'The poor man looks like he hasn't eaten for weeks.'

She stood by me until he came back, carrying the tea in front of him, two custard creams in the saucer. Dolly transferred the tea into my hands and stood over me as I took a sip. In the main hall they were singing another hymn.

'Listen to that,' she said. 'Isn't it grand? There's nothing I like better than hearing people sing. It does my heart good. Jim here's a wonderful baritone, Robert. He sang in the National Youth Choir when he was young, didn't you, Jim?'

Jim looked abashed.

'Go on. Of course you did. I know a singer when I hear one. They all said he'd turn professional one day. I don't know why he didn't. Crying shame, I call it, wasting talent like that. Just think, Jim, if you'd been a singer you could have been standing here selling your own records.'

She laughed heartily, and Jim gave a shy smile. I knew Dolly was trying to cheer me up so I smiled too, but it was the last thing I felt like doing. I hated hanging around. With nothing to do I found it harder to stave off the voices and control my nerves. In fact since talking to Joanna I had become so thoroughly depressed that I hardly knew what to do with myself. It might be another two hours before I met this Don Carroll, and even then

83

there was no guarantee that I wouldn't be misunderstood as I had been by the Catholics.

The amplified voice was speaking again in the hall. The hymn had been followed by the usual interlude of wriggling and coughing that precedes an address. Now the congregation was quiet. When Dolly opened the door to let someone in I could see the visitors in the back row staring thoughtfully ahead. They evidently found the talk interesting. I tried to pick up what the speaker was talking about, but his voice droned on with little change in pitch or expression and forty minutes later I hadn't caught more than a few words. It reminded me – simply because it was so unlike it – of Mrs Dawson's talk at the spiritist church. That had sparkled with fervour; so much so that it was hard to believe she was not telling the truth; by comparison this was as dry as dust. I couldn't work it out. Put in the position of this speaker – free of the evil spirits and restored to a normal, sane and healthy existence – I would be tossing my hat in the air and shouting that Jesus had saved me. To disbelieve in Jesus, or to loathe him as the Guide appeared to do, was at least consistent. But to be a Christian and take him for granted made no sense at all.

'More tea?' said Dolly, coming back from the doors, where she had been listening to the talk.

'No thank you. Is it going to be very much longer?'

'Shouldn't think so. He's done with speaking now, so it's just the last hymn and a closing prayer.'

I was relieved. I almost felt happy when the hymn finished and the conference broke up. But it took a long time for everyone to leave. Ten minutes after the end most people were still in the hall, talking. I watched the first few drift through the lobby in little groups of two or three, oblivious of anything but the conference and their own concerns. They took no notice of me. When the main part of the assembly left and Dolly was hidden behind a moving wall of bodies I felt as lonely as I had outside Holborn station. The most attention I got was a 'Sorry!' after someone trod on my foot.

At last the crowd thinned out, leaving a cold wind blowing in off the street. Dolly and Jim closed the doors and started picking up the litter of papers on the floor. I got up to stretch my legs. Sitting for so long had let fatigue get a firm grip on me, and I was beginning to feel very faint. I walked across the lobby and back again without seeing anyone but the ushers. It was all very quiet. I began to wonder if I hadn't been forgotten, and whether the Rev Carroll hadn't like everyone else gone off home to bed. It was five more minutes before I heard footsteps in the hall.

A moment later there came in not one minister, but seven, all wearing dog-collars, among them the curly-haired man I had met on Kingsway. His friend wasn't with him. They came straight over to me like a swarm of medical students round a patient's bed. The most senior of them, who I presumed to be Don Carroll, was speaking with the curly-haired minister. He nodded and smiled, then addressed me.

'So you're the chap with the problems, are you?' he beamed. 'Would you like to fill us in on what's happened to you?'

I did so at length. When I'd finished the man on Don Carroll's right whispered something in his ear. The Rev Carroll listened, then shook his head firmly.

'I'm sure I'm possessed,' I pleaded, thinking I might be sent off to see a doctor. 'I'm also sure that only Jesus can get rid of the evil spirits.'

The man who had been whispering said, 'I really think – ' but Don Carroll stopped him with a gesture. 'You're quite right, Mr Lee,' he said. 'Only Jesus can overcome the power of evil. And Jesus will assist us if we pray with faith. Now let's all of us join hands and stand in a circle.'

Silence fell. I realised I was starting to shake. The voices inside me were shouting with loud, inarticulate cries. Looking round the lobby I saw shadows moulding themselves into hideous, half-human, half-animal faces. I swallowed and closed my eyes, but they were still there, leering at me from the depths of my mind like living gargoyles. 'Jesus,' I moaned, 'help me, please!'

'Shut up!' spat a voice within. 'We're here, and we're staying. There's no use asking Jesus to help you. The only way you've used that name till now is to swear with it.'

My knees wanted to buckle, but the men at my sides grasped me strongly. Don Carroll started to pray. 'Our Lord Jesus,' he said, 'we ask you to hear our prayers for this afflicted one ... '

'No! No!' cried the voices.

' ... He has fallen under the power of evil and cannot tear himself away. But you, O Lord, have proven by your death and resurrection that the dominion is yours. As your word says, you have led death captive by the cross and triumphed over the powers of darkness. Therefore ... '

'Lies!' roared the voices. 'Our master rules and no one is greater than he!'

' ... we pray, O Lord, that in accordance with your might and power you will destroy the evil force that grips this man, and set him free.'

I heard a noise like a thunderclap and suddenly my head was filled with wild, bellowing cries. It was as if I had fallen into the middle of a pitched battle, and men were forcing their way past me, thrusting and hacking at each other and yelling for all they were worth. I was withdrawn from the everyday world in which a few seconds before I had been standing with the ministers, and was thrown headlong into confusion.

What made it so terrifying was the fact that I could only hear the turmoil around me, but not see it. Like a blind man my instinctive reaction was to duck before I was physically cut down. But, as sometimes happens in a nightmare, my body refused to obey the orders issued by the mind. The two seemed to occupy different worlds. The more I flinched or tried to dodge the blade I thought was swinging in my direction, the more obstinately my limbs stayed fixed in position. The feeling was quite uncanny. It was only at the very fringes of my consciousness that I still felt, faintly, the hard grip on my hands of the two ministers who stood beside me.

For a while the fighting grew steadily more intense. I couldn't see the combatants, but I pictured them as warriors in classical dress – only three or four times the size of ordinary men. Joanna, who had a great interest in the histories of Greece and Rome, had often described to me their weapons and methods of warfare. This produced in me a conviction that at any moment I would be run through, riddled with arrows, or simply trampled on. At the pinnacle of the battle I was squeezing my eyes tight closed and calling out miserably, in a voice I could hardly hear, 'Jesus, Jesus, Jesus ... '

At last the noise began to subside, as if the battle was surging off into another part of the field. I became aware that someone was praying. The words were smooth and quiet and strong, and when one voice left off another would take them up so that they made together a running stream of prayer. I had a profound sense of being at rest; the sort of feeling you get when after swimming in the ocean you lie down once again and sprawl luxuriously in the sunshine. Slowly, miraculously, the battle receded until even the loudest cries were lost in the distance, and I was surrounded by an unbroken circle of peace.

Silence fell, a cool, refreshing, delicious silence such as I had not experienced for months. I basked in it. The trickle of prayer had died away and I could hear nothing at all. The evil faces and my crude imaginations of battle had vanished. When finally I opened my eyes the only faces I saw were those of the seven ministers. Don Carroll was smiling broadly.

'Well, how do you feel?'

'Marvellous!' I said, hardly able to believe it.

There were smiles all round. 'God be praised,' said the Rev Carroll.

'But – will they come back?'

'The voices, you mean?' He shook his head. 'No. You have been under the influence of evil, and through prayer and the power of God you have been set free of it. Of course it is very important that you keep away from the things you have been involved in. You must make a clean break with all forms of evil. Such things are filthy in the eyes of God. So no more seances, and get rid of that ouija board. Your job from now on is to live as a Christian should.'

I must have looked perplexed, because he spread his arms out wide and said, 'Agreed?'

'Yes!' Everyone nodded in confirmation – everyone, I think, except the man who had been arguing with him at the start.

I gave in willingly and went forward, taking Don Carroll by the hand. 'Thank you so much. You can't appreciate how much this means to me.' He smiled and shrugged and said that all the credit was due to God. After that I went round the entire circle, shaking hands and flooding them with gratitude. They wished me well. When I came to the curly-haired minister I apologised for my behaviour on Kingsway and said, jokingly, that I hoped it wouldn't happen again. He laughed and agreed it wasn't likely to. He and his friend worked at churches in Birmingham and the chances of them being outside Holborn tube station in the next few years were extremely remote.

I was grinning helplessly. Suddenly I felt so happy I could hardly contain myself. It was over a year since I'd been free of the voices. To have peace restored to my mind so quickly and so dramatically made me feel like dancing for joy. I could not have been more exuberant if I'd been let off scot-free the hour before my execution. I imagined myself telling Joanna the next morning how Jesus had answered my prayer, and being reunited with my children and getting back into the swing of my old family life. The future broke on me like a glorious, fresh dawn.

In the end we were laughing and chatting like old schoolmates at a reunion. When Don Carroll cleared his throat loudly and announced that the caretaker wanted to lock up there was a distinct feeling that the party was being spoiled. But everyone started tucking their scarves into their coats and pulling on gloves, and one or two drifted towards the door.

'Can I offer anyone a lift?' I said. 'I'm driving back through Bethnal Green towards Enfield.'

Four people agreed, and waving our goodbyes we hurried down the steps to the street. Outside the rain was coming down steadily. Someone put up an umbrella and we huddled underneath it, splashing through the puddles as we went. We were all rather wet by the time we reached the car, which was parked where I'd left it on Holborn Circus. This caused my passengers great hilarity. One of them said that if they'd known I was a criminal they would never have let me into the conference.

'Right, who lives nearest?' I said as we clambered in.

'Mile End. Jays Crescent,' said one of the men in the back.

'No one lives nearer than that?'

No one did. I pulled the key from my pocket and said as I turned the ignition, 'Do you know, when I started the car this morning I was going to deliver a message for those voices.'

'For the last time,' said the man in the back. 'They're all gone now.'

'Yes,' I smiled.

'But then a cold sensation crept over my body, starting with my feet and spreading upwards as if I were being immersed in icy water. I shuddered. The man in the passenger seat saw me grimace and said, 'Are you all right?' But I hardly heard him. I was rigid, and when I spoke it wasn't in reply to his question. My attention was turned entirely inward. The oblong screen had appeared again and my hands felt light, as they had done earlier when I was writing. I began slowly shaking my head. 'No, please, no. I can't stand any more of it ... '

For I was hearing once again the voice of the Guide. He sounded maddened and punch-drunk, but no less vicious than before. I could feel him physically reasserting his control over me.

'You don't get rid of us that easily,' he hissed. 'And we've got you for certain this time ... '

7: The end of the trail

I switched off the engine and leapt against the door. 'They're still there!' I shouted. 'I can hear them!'

'Who, the voices?'

'Yes. I've got to get back and catch the Rev Carroll before he goes.'

I jumped out and ran across the street. We were some distance from the hall and I had to move fast. The rain was coming down heavily. Water ran deep along the gutters and was collecting in pools where the drains were blocked. Jumping one of these I misjudged my landing and got wet up to the ankle. The cold water stung and swilled in my shoe.

When I reached the City Temple the caretaker, who was in a long raincoat and trilby, was locking the last door.

'Is the Rev Carroll still here?' I said, breathlessly.

'Who?'

'Don Carroll, the man with the dog-collar and the black attaché case.'

'Oh, him,' said the caretaker. 'No, they've all gone.'

'How long ago?'

'I don't know. Five minutes, ten minutes. I wasn't timing them with a stopwatch, was I?'

'Where did he go? What direction?'

'Didn't see. I expect he took the tube; but then again he might have taken the bus, or he might have a car. I dare say a man like him would have a car, wouldn't you?'

'Yes, yes, of course,' I said irritably, 'but you think the tube is most likely?'

The man pursed his lips in a leisurely way.' 'Reckon your guess is as good as mine,' he said at last.

I looked up and down the street to discover some trace of the Rev Carroll. There was none. Two buses had stopped on the other side and were rumbling off into the distance, leaving behind a scatter of passengers, none of whom resembled the man I was looking for. If he was on one of the buses I'd missed him. Would he have gone on the tube? Perhaps, but he had a head start on me, and even if I bought a ticket and by good luck arrived on the right platform, the train might already have taken him away. That left the car. It was just possible that he had parked some way off and was walking slowly enough for me to catch up with him. But the chances of picking the right street in the labyrinthine back streets of London were a million to one. I might as well face up to it: Don Carroll had gone, and I was pretty well back where I'd started.

I took a deep breath, and glanced round at the caretaker. He was standing with his hands in his pockets, a faintly amused expression on his face.

'What are you going to do, then?' he said.

I didn't resent the question. He must have come across enough oddballs in a job like his — it was only natural he should think of me as another one.

'I don't know what I'm going to do,' I said, turning to leave. 'Pray for me.'

I left him staring after me as I trudged away. The rain had soaked through my jacket and shirt by now and I was starting to shiver. Most of those I passed quickened their step when they saw me. The accumulated fatigue of sleepless nights was creeping back; new hope had buoyed me up for a while, but now that the hope was exhausted I was coming down to earth again as swiftly as a punctured balloon. For some reason the prayer had failed. It might have knocked the voices out cold at first, but now they were picking themselves up off the boards to continue the fight. Their resources were boundless. You might suppress them or keep them at bay, but to get rid of them entirely was impossible.

'Why don't you give up?' said the Guide, suddenly.

I walked on, staring fixedly into the distance. 'Not yet,' I murmured. 'Not while I've strength left.'

'You won't last long now. Every second you delay will only

make your punishment worse.'

'Jesus will help me.'

The Guide laughed. It was a harsh, forced laugh. 'Help you? How's he going to do that?'

'He gave you a beating this evening. He'll do it again.'

'Not such a beating as we're going to give you when you stop all this foolishness.'

'Oh, shut up!'

'Of course,' the Guide went on blithely. 'you know why those ministers weren't able to help you?'

I didn't answer.

'It's because they thought you were a good man.' I heard a chorus of spiteful laughter. 'Imagine that. You, a good man! They must be suckers. You came crawling to them, wanting to get rid of us. But did you let on how evil you really are? Not likely! They'd have flung you back out on the street.'

As a matter of fact they were right. I hadn't said anything to the Presbyterians about the life I'd led before getting into spiritism. Somehow it hadn't seemed important. To be seeking help from Jesus after rejecting him for most of my life had surely been an adequate demonstration of my sincerity. And, anyway, underneath it all I really was sorry for what I'd done. I'd said as much to the Catholic priest. 'You're lying,' I said, flatly.

There was no response. Only the persistent muttering and scheming I had been used to for the last year or so. Whether the remark was true or not they had decided to let me chew on it. I did so, and eventually decided that anything the voices told me must necessarily be false, and tried to put it out of my mind. I almost succeeded.

Back at the car three of my passengers had gone. The only one left was sitting in the front seat, a small, black Bible open on his knees. He had introduced himself to me earlier as Mr Price, a shy, soft-spoken man in late middle age. He looked up as I arrived, slumping into the driving seat and staring disconsolately at the streaming windscreen.

'Any luck?' he said.

I shook my head. 'I suppose you don't know where he lives?'

'I'm sorry, I don't.'

There was a pause.

'What happened to the rest of them?' I asked, listlessly.

'They opted for the tube. They asked me to convey their apologies.'

'Accepted,' I said with a shrug. 'I'm surprised you didn't go with them. Do you really want to drive home with a man possessed of evil spirits? I might go berserk and drive off a bridge.'

'I trust Jesus,' said Mr Price, quietly.

I turned the ignition, and the engine roared into life. 'OK, where do you live?'

'Ilford,' he said. Then with a twinkle in his eye he added, 'But we'll go to Hainault first of all.'

I looked at him in surprise. He had said it without any sort of emphasis, as if Hainault were the most obvious place to go at ten-thirty on a Tuesday night.

'And what's in Hainault?' I said, stupidly.

Mr Price gave a slight smile. 'A friend of mine. He has a gift of healing, and he might just be able to help you.'

So we went to Hainault. It is a suburb of the city, not far from my home in Loughton. I went with mixed feelings. On the one hand I was glad of another chance to get free of the voices. On the other, the word 'healing' had bad connotations for me, of my own former ambition and of a fruitless visit to the Spiritist Centre at Amersham Place, and the prospect of seeing another healer made me uneasy.

We said little until our arrival in Hainault made it necessary for Mr Price to give more detailed directions. We went under the railway bridge and took the first right turn, stopping a short distance along. Mr Price got out. The house he took me to was a three-bedroom semi of the sort that were built in thousands between the wars. Light glowed through the curtains in the front room.

'He's still up,' said Mr Price, knocking.

The man who opened the door had a thin, silver beard and was holding two empty mugs in his hand. He squinted at us and said, 'John! Come in, come in. What a surprise!'

We filed into the narrow hallway. A woman appeared, carrying a tray of dishes, and greeted us. From the room out of which she had come I heard laughter and the squawking of a television set.

'I hope we're not disturbing you, Harry,' said Mr Price.

'No, no. The family's here for the week. Pity you didn't come earlier. You could have met my grandchildren. Goodness, it's all go, isn't it? What can I do for you?'

Mr Price looked a bit anxious. 'If it's not too inconvenient, I'd like your help,' he said, and started, between bouts of laughter from the front room, to explain my problem. Harry listened attentively. I found myself watching his eyes, which pinched closed in an attitude of concentration. He had a kind face, a face accustomed to smiling. In a rather childish way I felt drawn to him. The house itself, which was so ordinary and prosaic, breathed a peace and safety I'd never known in my own home. I let it soak into me as the two men talked.

Eventually Harry turned to me. 'Would you like to come through to the back?' he said.

We followed him through a glass sliding door into a room with French windows and a plain, tiled fireplace. There was an assortment of blue china on the mantelpiece, and above them a faded print of the *Haywain*. Most of the floorspace was taken up with an oval dining table. Harry pushed this aside and we sat down.

'Now, Mr Lee,' he said, 'you'll have to excuse the cramped conditions. My son and daughter-in-law are watching the box next door, otherwise we could have gone in there.'

I hadn't noticed till then that he had a faint, Irish accent. He went on, 'Now, it goes without saying that if I'm going to pray for you, you must observe a few simple ground rules. First, do you believe in the Lord Jesus?'

'Yes.'

'And do you really want him to help you?'

'Yes. I'm desperate.'

'Good.' Harry laid a hand on my knee. 'Then you must pray out loud for the Lord Jesus to heal you and after that concentrate as hard as you can on letting him do it. There's nothing to be accomplished by prayer without your co-operation. When I put my hands on your head and ask God's healing power to come down on you, just say in your heart, "Thank you, Lord", and believe it's being done.'

'Will I feel anything, like a burning inside?'

The two men looked at me quizzically.

'I thought that was the way healing happened – someone tried to heal me before and it happened like that. It got so painful in the end I almost asked him to stop.'

'That was a spiritist healer?' said Harry.

'Yes. Up at Amersham Place.'

He shook his head. 'That kind of healing never helped anybody. Most times folk get sent away worse than they came in. That's because they don't believe in the Lord Jesus. They run around everywhere looking for someone to sort out their problems, and no one can. There's cancer victims, schizophrenics, people infected with evil like you. Every ailment under the sun, and they can't do a thing about it. They go on getting more and more desperate until it's a shame to look at them. And all because they won't come to the Lord Jesus. One word from him and they'd be healed on the spot.'

I listened to the angry murmur of the voices inside me. They were as restless as the wind, mustering that final blast that would push me over the brink of sanity. It was incredible to me now that I had ever been in league with these creatures, that I had sought their assistance in making me a healer. All the partnership had done was to put me in need of healing myself.

'Will Jesus heal *me?*' I said, casting an imploring look at Harry.

'We'll ask him.'

He reached down a book from the shelf and creased it open on his lap. 'Let's pray,' he said, breathing deeply, his eyes already closed. We followed suit, and for a moment waited in silence. I expected the sound inside me to rise to a crescendo as it had before I was prayed for in the City Temple. But the voices only kept up their banter, like troops engaged in digging a trench. When, on Harry's instructions, I prayed in a quivering voice for Jesus to heal me, their tone grew harsher but no louder. I reached the end of the prayer and swallowed hard. Harry and Mr Price said nothing. There was a pause of the sort that occurs in a mine before someone presses the plunger and blows the pit face sky high. Then I felt the light touch of Harry's fingers on my head, and he began to pray.

It didn't work. The two men laboured at their prayers for half an hour without any discernible result. The whole time that I was crouched on the chair obediently muttering my thanks to God they assailed the voices but did not dislodge them. It was as if the voices were too well dug in. The image that kept on

returning to my mind was that of a vast boulder. Two figures
were straining against it, trying to lever it out of its place and set
it rolling. But they could never quite manage to do it. Every time
they gained a purchase on it and lifted it off the ground their
strength gave way and it slumped back in its hole. In the end they
seemed to admit defeat and flopped down, leaning against it.

'No good,' said Harry, standing up.

We watched him frowning, one index finger to his lips.
'What's the hitch?' said Mr Price.

'I don't know. I'm sure we've done all the right things.'

'Has this happened before?'

'No. I can't make it out.'

I looked on miserably. 'I did what you told me,' I said.

'I know,' said Harry with a brief smile, 'I'm sorry we've run
into this little problem.'

There was a soft knock at the door, and the woman we'd seen
in the hall — Harry's wife — poked her head around it. 'Excuse
me,' she said. 'Harry, I'm off to bed. Would you have a look at
that toaster before you come up? It's burning the bread to
cinders and we need it for breakfast tomorrow.'

Harry nodded, and we all said good-night to her.

'Well ... ' Mr Price began.

I realised that this was the auspicious moment to leave. It was
a working day tomorrow, and I still had to take Mr Price back to
his home in Ilford. He had done what he was able; I couldn't
expect him to take me to yet another person in the hope that this
time something would shift. At the same time, if I dropped him
off and drove back to Loughton, alone, what would become of
me then?

'Well,' Mr Price said again, 'there's clearly no more to be done
tonight. I'm afraid we've drawn a blank, Mr Lee. Perhaps ... ' He
looked speculatively at Harry. 'Perhaps something could be
fixed up for tomorrow evening ...?'

They started discussing possible arrangements, but they
couldn't agree. I felt a sort of mental numbness come over me as
the prospect of my return to Loughton became more and more
inevitable. The past day now seemed like an enormous dream
that was steadily and inexorably drawing to a close. When I
stepped into my bedroom at home I would wake up.

'I'm sorry,' I broke in, 'but I really don't want to go home tonight. I'm going to go crazy if I do. The voices will attack me and I don't have the strength to stand up to them. I know it's rude of me to ask, but could I possibly stay here? I feel so safe here. I wouldn't be any trouble. I'd be happy sleeping on the floor in the hall ... '

Harry looked uncomfortable. Mr Price interposed for him. 'We can't ask Harry to put you up for the night, Mr Lee. He has his grandchildren to think of, and anyway we've intruded on him enough as it is. We really should go.'

I didn't argue. I hadn't known either man more than two hours, and I had no right to make demands of them. We said our goodbyes and, thanking Harry for his kindness, I stepped reluctantly out of the house. The cold enveloped us. My clothes were still damp from the rain earlier in the evening, and I shivered as I unlocked the car. The rain had eased off to a persistent drizzle without any change in the temperature.

We returned to Ilford on practically deserted roads. I was in no hurry to arrive, wanting to put off as long as possible the moment when I would be on my own again, and we crawled most of the way at 25 miles an hour. Once I almost fell asleep at the wheel and woke with a start. Mr Price did not stir; he was sitting quietly watching the street-lamps glide past, occasionally clearing his throat. If I'd had any energy left his composure might have annoyed me. To coolly take his leave when he knew full well what straits I was in was nothing short of callous.

Mr Price lived on Old Wells Road. As we drew up I heard a distant clock strike midnight. It rang all twelve chimes before either of us spoke. From one of the horror stories I had read at the Guide's behest came the memory that this was the witching hour. Mankind might rule the day; but night belonged to the Devil.

'You've been very kind,' I said, in a neutral tone.

'Not at all,' said Mr Price.

I wanted to detain him, keep him talking for just a little bit longer. 'I suppose I shan't be seeing you again. I doubt whether I'll get through tonight. I don't know why Jesus didn't want me – it seems to have been such an effort chasing round after him. All a bit of a waste of time, really.'

'God's time is never wasted,' said Mr Price. He climbed out of the car, straightened, then leaned back in, a small slip of paper in his hand. 'One of my colleagues gave me this,' he said. 'He told me you were possessed of evil spirits and that, if you hadn't been set free by the time I left you I should give you his telephone number. He's at home with friends praying for you now. If you want you can go and see them.'

I stared stupidly at the note. When I didn't take it Mr Price laid it on the seat. 'Good-night,' he said, closing the door.

Out of the corner of my eye I saw him go through an iron gate, up the path, and vanish into his house. I picked up the note. Sure enough there was a telephone number. Who on earth would be up praying for me at midnight? I stared at the figures. The exchange was in Watford – about 30 miles away. It seemed like a billion light years. So far every encounter I'd had today had done no more than provide a clue to the next. Was I really going to find Jesus, or did the chain go on for ever? It might, in the end, still turn out to be another mean trick on the part of the Guide. But no, I had to believe the clues were leading me somewhere. At any rate, if I didn't follow this one up, there was only one alternative. I crammed the note into my breast pocket and drove off.

Pendragon was dark and silent when I got back. I opened the door quietly and stood at the end of the hall. There was enough light filtering in from the street to see the table with yesterday's newspapers lying on top, and beyond it the staircase leading up into darkness. The family was asleep. But there were other beings present who never slept, who worked into the early hours to do their master's bidding. A strange feeling came over me. I was tired to the point of almost total exhaustion. It would be the easiest thing in the world to submit and walk up that staircase and let them have their way with me. They were urging me to do it. I would only have to step into that bedroom and I would be theirs – not because they were waiting to ambush me there, for they lived in my own body, but because my obedience would signify that I was giving myself up.

For a few seconds I gazed, stupefied, at the stairs. The voices were enticing me, drawing me on. I could hear the Guide among them. 'Go on,' they were saying, 'there's no use in resisting any further. Return to your master, the Devil.' I felt myself swaying towards the end of the hall, and with an effort of the will checked the motion. The voices faded a little.

I picked up the phone and dialled carefully. My sense of time had become distorted, for someone was speaking from the receiver before I had raised it to my ear.

'Hello. Yes? Hello?'

I stammered into the mouthpiece.

'Hello? Are you the man who was at the City Temple?'

'Yes,' I replied.

'We're waiting for you. Can you drive over?'

'Yes ... yes!' I said, recovering. 'Where are you?'

'Alexandria Road in Watford. The house is called *The Manse*.'

'I'm coming right now.'

'Good. We're praying for you.'

I put the receiver back. So there really *was* someone waiting up to help me! I felt like laughing and crying at the same time, so delicately was I poised between hope and desperation. I prayed under my breath, 'Please, Jesus, let it be real this time. I can't bear to be tricked again ... ' Then I shook off my wet jacket, threw an overcoat on my shoulders and stumbled out to the car. The engine was still running. I revved it loudly and jerked backwards out of the drive.

Before I reached the first bend in the road I heard the snarling voice of the Guide.

'Get back in the house, you fool. Do you think you can escape us now?'

I didn't answer.

'How are you going to get to Watford in your condition? You're practically in a coma, you're so tired. You'll drive off the road and kill yourself.'

'Jesus, let me get there', I whispered.

'Stop snivelling. I've told you Jesus can't help you now.'

Behind the Guide's voice there were others, a whole crowd of them, screaming threats and insults. If I didn't drive through a crash barrier myself I wondered whether they wouldn't do the job for me. Just listening to them made my blood run cold.

'I'm going,' I said, my voice shaking uncontrollably, 'I'm going, and you won't stop me.'

'We don't have to stop you,' jeered the Guide. 'Nothing's going to happen when you get there. You've been prayed for twice already, and what good has it done you? None. We're too strong to be affected by a few feeble prayers.'

'Jesus,' I whimpered. 'Jesus, Jesus ... '

'Jesus won't lift a finger to save you. You must be a fool if you're pinning your hopes on that. You're too evil. All Jesus would do if he saw you is throw you into hell. That's where you belong – in hell, with us. Why do you think we were able to beat off the prayers of those Presbyterians? Because you're evil. Why did that healer fail to help you? Because you're evil. Why did the priest at the Catholic church refuse to hear your confession? It was because he knew how evil you were and he didn't want to contaminate himself by listening to you. Face it, Robert, you're damned.'

I shook my head tearfully. 'No ... no!'

But the whole chorus of voices had joined in by now, and the entire bloodthirsty mob was shouting, 'Damned! Jesus doesn't want you! You're damned!'

The sheer bedlam of the voices threatened to engulf me as it had at the City Temple. My will to go on was being sapped dry. I was out of the city now and driving alone into total darkness. There were no street-lamps, not even any stars. I began to fear that some insane magic had swept me off the face of the earth, that the road skimming beneath me was an illusion and I was really fleeing deeper into the darkness of hell.

I lifted one hand off the wheel and slapped myself on the cheek in an attempt to snap back to reality. My mind registered a brief spasm of pain but the hallucination failed to break. It was like being caught up in a huge fairground ride, sensing a violent motion sickness and moving so fast that the familiar shouts and carnival music were warped out of recognition. There was nothing I could do to stop it. I could only hope I wouldn't pass out and run the car off the road. Dizzily I fixed my gaze on the cat's-eyes racing towards me out of the night. They rushed up and out of sight like shooting stars or anti-aircraft flak. Having no other way to retain my concentration I started, mechanically, to count them.

I don't know what number I had reached when at last the pressure began to ease and I returned to something resembling normal consciousness. I was still travelling, immensely tired but awake. It was almost as if I'd awoken on a fresh and superior level of awareness, because although my thought was faint with exhaustion it was at the same time incredibly clear. I took stock of my situation. I knew I'd been on the run, looking for Jesus and twice almost escaping from the evil spirits that gripped me. Both times the prayer had failed. Was it that the voices were too strong to be moved by that sort of prayer? I didn't know. But something that the Guide said had stuck in my mind: *You belong with us in hell.*

When he said it I had tried to contradict him, but I knew with a perfect surety that he was right. The reason why these evil spirits were able to occupy my body was that there was something evil about my own nature. We were of the same substance. I had noted earlier several of my past actions that marked me out as a man who had rejected God, and lamented them. But somehow I had not managed to shake them off. They encumbered me like a lead weight fastened to my ankles. What was I going to do?

There was really only one option. I would do at Watford what I had not done before the last two sessions of prayer: I would tell the ministers what I was really like. The prospect chilled me. According to the voices the priest at the Catholic church had wanted to get away from me because I was so evil. Might I not be slitting my own throat by admitting it now? I suppressed the thought. If they rejected me, so be it. I knew I had to speak out. If I didn't, their prayer would probably be useless anyway.

Suddenly lights appeared on the horizon. I looked out for a sign and soon found one. This was Watford. I had got here even though for most of the journey I had no idea where I was going. I gripped the wheel harder.

'Go back!' hissed the Guide. 'Do you want to get killed?'

The car ploughed on into the sleeping town. I was on a main road with terraced housing on either side. None of the street names were familiar. I came to an empty crossroads and stopped at the red light.

'Jesus, show me where to go,' I prayed under my breath.

'There's nowhere to go!' came a voice. 'You're a fool driving round like this. We'll make sure you never find your way.'

Impulsively I swung round to the left then took a couple of turns at random. This brought me into a side street with grass verges and trees. I peered out for the name and discovered to my surprise that I was in Daffodil Road. The sound in my head rose to a storm. I had to slow down and blink to disperse the pain.

The houses crawled by. I counted off the numbers until I came to a gate bearing no number, only a name. I looked closer. *The Manse.* Beyond it was a large building with a light on in the front, downstairs room.

'Drive on! Drive on!' the voices shrieked.

I braked with a jolt and flung open the door.

'Drive on, you wretch! Get away from here!'

But I was already out of the car and running, my hands over my ears, to the front door. I hammered loudly. As soon as it opened I plunged in and slumped against a wall, trying to catch my breath.

'Glad you made it,' said the man inside, a rather well-built gentleman in his shirt-sleeves. 'I'm Mr Barrow.'

He took me into a large room where the embers of a fire were smoking in the hearth. A few old, covered armshairs were drawn up around it and some empty coffee cups sat on a small, oak table. Much of the wall space was taken up by photographs of Boys Brigade companies and soccer teams. The place had a comfortable, well-worn look about it.

The other men stood up when I came in and were introduced as Mr Brideswell, a Presbyterian minister, and Mr Williams, a lay worker from Mr Barrow's church.

'We prayed for you to have a safe journey,' said Mr Brideswell.

'Not easy, driving with demons,' Mr Barrow observed. 'It's a curious fact, but I knew you were possessed the moment I saw you at the City Temple.'

I recognised him then as the man who had argued before the prayer session. 'Is that what you were trying to tell the Rev Carroll?' I asked.

'Yes, that's right. He wouldn't listen. Little fish can't tell the big fish what to do, even in the church, Mr Lee.'

I smiled nervously. I felt tremendous strength being here with these men.

It was as if Jesus himself were standing, unseen, in the room. At the same time I had the uncomfortable conviction that I was an impostor. In a purely physical way I could feel the presence of evil within me. My guts seemed to be full of writhing snakes; they were wrestling for position, awaiting the chance to strike. In this warm, pleasant household I was causing a sort of spiritual pollution.

Mr Barrow rubbed his hands together amiably. 'Well, I think we'd better get started ... '

'Wait,' I said hurriedly, then paused, fingering the wing of an armchair. 'I decided on the way over here that there's something you ought to know about me.'

Mr Barrow raised his eyebrows.

'I wasn't going to say anything,' I went on, 'but I want to make it clear I'm not a church-goer. I'm not even a very good man by ordinary standards, though I've always taken care to look respectable on the outside. Hidden away inside me there's a lot I'm pretty ashamed of ... '

I began telling them about my dishonest fiddling at work, my arrogance and my secret addiction to pornographic literature. When that was done, other things came to mind. The list slowly got longer and longer. The evil part of my nature was like the hydra: where one head was cut off there immediately appeared two more to take its place. I suddenly discovered that my life was chock-full of wrongdoing. Actions I'd forgotten and actions I'd carried out in comparative innocence now returned in their blackest aspect. It was horrific to hear myself recounting them all, and yet I couldn't stop. I had to go on pouring it all out to the bitter end. At one stage I panicked and looked frantically from one man to the other, certain that they were about to throw me out. But they said nothing, and on it went until finally I choked on my words and fell silent, shaking slightly, my eyes averted.

Mr Williams cleared his throat. He then opened his Bible and said, 'Mr Lee, it tells us in God's word, "If we confess our sins, he is faithful and just, and will forgive our sins and cleanse us from all unrighteousness." All of us have done things we're ashamed of. These things are called "sins" in the Bible, and they separate us from God. But if we admit that we've done them – if we *confess* them – God will forgive us and forgo the punishment we deserve.' He smiled. 'Don't worry. You did the right thing telling us about them. You have confessed them to us and to God, and God has most certainly forgiven you. All that remains is to set you free of the Devil.'

Mr Barrow beckoned me to kneel down at the far end of the room, where there was a small altar. I got down on my knees and watched the candle flame dancing over the purple cloth. A peace had descended on me. It was as if a weight I'd been staggering about with for years had been suddenly lifted from my shoulders. I knew what it was, too: the same 'sin' that old Mr Hartley had warned me about back in 1928. How I had failed to grasp its meaning was incredible to me now. Looking back it was painfully obvious how, after shrugging off God and the Devil as myths, I had fallen straight into it. What a fool – but no, it was all dealt with now. I closed my eyes and heaved a sigh of relief.

Mr Williams, who had come up behind me, laid a hand on my shoulder. 'Think of Jesus, Mr Lee,' he said. 'You may remember that when those possessed of evil spirits came to him he cast out the spirits with a single word.'

I did remember. Curiously, I had Bastion House to thank for that; for all his apparent failings the headmaster had one redeeming quality: he believed in giving his pupils a Christian education. We had Bible readings as a regular part of our study.

'And what Jesus did then,' Mr Williams continued, 'he gives his followers the authority to do now.'

Inside me the voices were screaming with meaningless, bestial cries. I couldn't distinguish one from another. They seemed to have degenerated into anarchy and to be fighting among themselves. All I sensed was a violent anger – against God, against Jesus, against the men in the room, against me. The physical symptoms were now so clear that I could have sworn my intestines were twisting round inside me. My right hand trembled and the screen in my mind was projecting harsh, rapidly changing patterns across my vision. I tried to think of the scene Mr Hartley had described, where Jesus confronted the Devil in the wilderness. Three times the Devil tempted him, and three times Jesus argued the Devil down. A feeling of nausea came over me.

Mr Williams took a deep breath and said in a loud, authoritative tone, 'Satan, I bind you in the name of the Lord Jesus Christ. And I command every evil spirit in this man to come out now, in the name of Jesus!'

The spirits gave me one last convulsive wrench. As Mr Williams spoke I sensed a turmoil within me like the drawing up of a wave in the instant before it breaks. Then, as if a great fist had reached down into my innermost being, I felt the evil spirits ripped out of me. I gave a cry and toppled backwards ...

The Devil had departed.

8: The new man

I felt a pair of hands grasping my shoulders. They belonged to
Mr Williams, who had held me when I lost my balance. The
other men were crouching down in front of me. Mr Barrow had
taken hold of my arm.

'Are you all right?' he said.

'Yes ... yes.'

'Have the voices gone?'

I began to collect my wits. Within my mind there was a sense
of complete calm; not just an absence of noise and activity, but
something positive, like a still day in midsummer.

'Yes,' I sighed, 'they've gone.'

I was absolutely certain of it. No doubt lingered in my mind as
it had done at the City Temple. I was able to look at myself as a
man might look over a newly decorated house and find every
room bright and fresh, with the windows thrown open to greet
the new day. Not the slightest murmur remained in my head.
The oblong screen that had scarred my vision had flickered and
gone out like a candle. Flexing my fingers I found them to be
wholly under my own control. I was free.

Suddenly my heart could have broken with gratitude. I made
no attempt to conceal my feelings. 'Thank you, Jesus,' I said my
voice wavering with emotion. 'Oh, thank you so, so much.'

The tension that had been building up during the course of
the day had finally snapped. I had begun my quest almost as a
reflex reaction – an anguished plea for help; I had ended it a
changed man. Time and again I had experienced disappointment. At first it had been the disappointment of a gambler,
defeated simply by the laws of chance. But when on the drive

to Watford I had contemplated a last and conclusive failure I had done so in a state of penitence. I knew that if the prayer failed and I was abandoned to the Devil it would be no more than I had deserved.

'Why did he do it?' I said. 'Why did Jesus do it?'

Mr Barrow smiled. 'Because he loves you.'

'But I don't deserve it. I hated him for thirty years. I wouldn't even let my children go to Sunday school.'

'If God treated us all as we deserve,' said Mr Barrow, 'we'd be in a fine mess. It's the first step in being a Christian to realise we don't deserve anything.'

'But how could he love *me*?'

'God loves his enemies,' replied Mr Barrow, simply. 'No one is too evil for God to love them — even Stalin. He's always looking for opportunities to reach them, make them change their ways. And if they do he gives them a completely fresh start — just as he's doing for you.'

'I closed my eyes. The truth was starting to unfold before me in a way I had never known until now. I had always taken it for granted that my outlook on life was generally the 'right' one and regarded Christianity as a crude, medieval belief fit only for inadequates and fanatics. In that way I had made myself God's enemy — no doubt with some encouragement from the Devil. It flattered my pride to put religion down. But the war on God was one that I had no chance of winning; in fact it wasn't really a war at all because God didn't regard me as *his* enemy (he probably didn't have any) but as someone lost and in need of help. The fact I was still alive and in my right mind was due solely to God's love.

Behind me I felt Mr Williams get to his feet. The other two followed suit. They stood in silence for a while before Mr Barrow said gently, 'Well, Mr Lee, I think you had better be getting home. You've a long way to go, and you must be very tired.'

'Yes, of course.'

I rose, and clasped their hands warmly. I was very tired — so tired that I could cheerfully have laid down on the floor and slept through into the afternoon. I summoned what words I could string together to express my gratitude to Mr Barrow and his friends for their assistance to me. That too had been undeserved. The three men accepted my thanks gracefully. Like me, they looked exhausted; while I was driving around the city they had been on their knees in prayer.

Soon we were at the door and saying our goodbyes. The night air felt cold on my face as I stepped outside. It was a gentle reminder of the colder spiritual forces that had only a few minutes before been living within me. I glanced back at Mr Barrow. 'Don't worry,' he said. 'Jesus has set you free. You'll be in no danger from the Devil on your way home. Just drive carefully.'

The door closed.

I turned, and summoning my courage began to walk down the path to the gate. When I reached it I paused, listening. I was certain I'd heard a noise in the darkness beside me, the sort of noise a twig makes when someone steps on it. I peered into the black square in front of the house which in daylight would have appeared as a lawn or a rose garden. No movement. I hesitated, afraid to stay and afraid to go on. I fully believed that Jesus had driven the Guide and the other voices out of my body – but where were they now? The thought suddenly struck me that they might be waiting in the shadows outside the house, or hiding in the car.

I ran back to the door and rapped loudly. Mr Barrow answered.

'I'm scared,' I said, looking at him plaintively. 'Are you sure the spirits are really gone? They couldn't be out here ready to possess me again?'

He smiled. 'No. Your spirits have gone for ever. And even if they hadn't it would make no difference. They have no more power to harm you now than they did when they were cast out.'

'But I'm on my own now.'

'Nonsense', he boomed. 'Christians are never alone. Jesus is with them wherever they find themselves. And if Jesus is with you, there's nothing the Devil can do about it.'

I nodded silently. I believed him, but I was still afraid.

'Now,' said Mr Barrow, 'drive back, and trust in the power of Jesus.'

Once again I walked away down the path. This time I reached the car before coming back.

On my second return Mr Barrow was much firmer. 'Look,' he said, 'you're afraid because of the darkness. One of the things the Bible says about Jesus is that he is the Light. And where there's light, the darkness has to go. You wouldn't be half as scared if it was broad daylight out there, would you? No. Then go out knowing that the Light is with you. From now on, if you meet the Devil or his spirits, remember that Light. The Devil will run from it.'

The door closed for the third and final time, and I turned to face the night. I sincerely hoped I was going to meet neither the Devil nor his spirits. Right then I felt like a man lost overboard from a ship: I had escaped drowning, but I still faced a long and stormy swim to the shore. All my instincts told me that concealed beneath the frothy waves were rocks. It was going to require more strength than I possessed to get through the next hour.

I walked hastily back to the Consul and turned the ignition. So far so good: no spectres had leapt out at me from the darkness. None the less there was around me an unmistakable sense of cold; not physical cold, though the air was distinctly chilly. It touched me in my emotions. I imagined myself suspended above an icy cold sea, hanging on to a long slender thread. This thread was the only thing that prevented my plunging into the water beneath. Under my breath I prayed, 'Jesus, I'm grasping my end as hard as I can. Please don't let go of yours!'

The journey back to Enfield was better than the journey out only because I didn't have the voices yelling in my ears. But I felt more exhausted, and three times almost drove off the road when I fell asleep. On each occasion I managed to struggle back to semi-consciousness just in time to correct the steering. But it was a close shave. When I arrived at the house I was literally sobbing with gratitude that I was still alive.

I dragged myself out of the car and into the house. *Pendragon* was the same as it had been when I left it at about one o'clock in the morning. Three hours had passed since then. I leaned against the front door to shut it and remained there staring wearily down the hall. Ahead of me were the stairs, just as dark as they had been before. They no longer exerted any alluring power over me, but I found nevertheless that I was unwilling to mount them. This darkness, this terror of my own bedroom where so much of my suffering had taken place, was the last hurdle on the track. Forcing myself, I removed my overcoat and went up.

Joanna was breathing lightly as I entered the room. She didn't stir. I looked into the dark corners, half expecting to glimpse a figure or a faint glimmer of the oblong screen. There was nothing; only the glow of the street-lamp through the curtains. I undressed, sitting down on the edge of the bed. On the bedside table was the bottle of sleeping pills I had touched in the morning in my search for the alarm clock. I took it in my hand and realised that for the first time in months I wasn't going to need the little green and white capsules. Staying awake would have been more impossible to me now than sleeping. Setting the tablets down I rolled back into the bed and pulled the covers round me. 'Thank you, Jesus,' I whispered, 'I don't know why you love me like this. But thank you.' In a matter of seconds I was asleep.

The whole process of my deliverance had taken just over twelve hours. No doctors or psychiatrists had played a part in it. I had simply been prayed for and had the evil spirits pulled out of me. From that moment on my life changed; but not back to the old, safe atheistic mould in which I had cast myself before. I felt as if I'd been given a new lease on life – in fact as if I'd received a completely new kind of life. A life directed and empowered by Jesus. Of course the fear and the fatigue didn't fall away immediately. For a long time the only thing I wanted to do with my past was to get as far away from it as I could. Not for me the Devil's temptations in the wilderness. I would have been happy enough for all knowledge of the Devil to be erased from my memory. It would have shocked me then to know that I was one day to meet the Devil's forces again – in a very different way.

Of the days that followed the deliverance little can be said here. I began learning how to be a follower of Jesus. This was a stark contrast to the training the Guide had given me. The themes of fear and coercion gave way to a new theme – of thanksgiving to God for what he had done. There were problems and challenges, of course. For instance, I found when I started attending St Anselm's that not one member – including the vicar – could believe I had been possessed of evil spirits. My story was invariably received with embarrassed looks or hasty attempts to change the subject. Their attitude perplexed me. It appeared that the Christians I had met at Watford were an exception to the general rule and that I had been extremely fortunate to find them.

A more pressing difficulty arose at home. After my own conversion I realised the appalling danger into which I had led the family by my devotion to spiritism. I myself had been saved from the consequences by the skin of my teeth. Naturally I felt it my duty to safeguard my wife and children. The very next morning after the deliverance I got up and made the coffee, and brought it upstairs to Joanna to tell her what had happened. I explained how Jesus had finally set me free from the spirit voices, and that I had been converted; I apologised for misleading her by my investigation of spiritism, emphasised how dangerous it was, and begged her to join me in becoming a Christian.

She wouldn't. And in spite of all my efforts she stuck by her decision in the years that followed. Partly, this was because my conversion must have appeared from the outside as a slow process. Long after I had recovered from the physical and psychological shock of my experience I was struggling to overcome the unpleasant traits in my nature that I now knew were wrong. I still got angry. I still refused to listen. And none of that helped to restore Joanna's faith in me. To her, Christianity was the last in a series of my 'big ideas', another fanatical craze that she wanted nothing to do with. As a result my frequent and conscience-stricken preaching served only to widen the gulf I had introduced by my obedience to the spirits. That was painful for both of us; but I could see no way across it.

Time went by. Miraculously, I had come through the entire, traumatic sequence of spirit possession and conversion without missing a single day at work, and the suspicions roused in my colleagues were soon laid to rest. Not long after I received a further promotion, to the managerial level, and settled back into the routine of daily life, trying as best I could to live as a Christian and to forget the experience I'd gone through.

In an effort to express some of my gratitude to God I began to take up voluntary work. One of the first things I did was join the Samaritans, a service that provides a listening ear for those under stress or on the verge of suicide. It was through this organisation, in the late 1960s, that I met Tom Marriott, and became involved with his scheme for the rehabilitation of drug addicts at Portal House in Romford. Tom was for me a very charismatic figure; he seemed to embody the sort of openness and enthusiasm that I felt Christians really ought to have but which, in most places where I found them, they lacked. Gradually I spent more and more of my spare time on Tom's project, and learned a lot working alongside him until he moved away to start another scheme in rural Essex.

About this time two crises occurred. First, I lost my job. In 1970 there was a reshuffle in the industry and I was given an early retirement. This was swiftly followed by a far more painful blow. Joanna's health began to deteriorate. In a way it was providential that I was no longer working, since I was able to nurse her. But her condition slowly worsened, and in March, 1972, after two major operations, she died. Being forewarned by the doctors did little to soften the shock when it came. Our marriage had on the whole been a very happy one, and in spite of the estrangement over my spiritist phase and conversion the grief I felt at losing her was profound. It was a long time before I could see, beside the grief, the chance of a new beginning.

In the following five years several things happened, which can only be mentioned very briefly. I started helping, in an unofficial way, at Trevor Dearing's church in Hainault. At the time there was a lot of interest in the media about the miraculous healings and deliverances that were taking place there. My part in the ministry of the church was very small, but when Trevor left to form the independent Power, Praise and Healing Mission I made myself available to help him. I hadn't taken up another job, and I had plenty of time on my hands.

In many ways I felt very lonely. True, there was a lot of work to keep me occupied and I had a lot of friends, but at home only my younger son, David, remained, and he was as often as not out of the house. It came as both a surprise and a joy when I met Bella, and I realised I was to be married again. This seemed a full compensation for the misery I'd received from the Devil. Even the house was transformed – it was rather appropriate that a short while before the wedding I renamed it *Hallelujah!*

It is since our wedding that our ministry has begun to unfold. I don't mean ministry in the sense of my being an ordained clergyman. The word can be used by any Christian for the special work God has given him or her to do. In our case the work has revolved around our home. We occasionally go out to take part in missions and church meetings, but most of the time we find people phoning us to ask if they can come over and be prayed for. They have a wide variety of problems – few of which we have the technical qualifications to solve – but if they are looking for Jesus in the way that I was back in 1961 we find that, in a remarkable way, God is able to use us to help them out.

But that is getting ahead of the story.

It was in my early days at Portal House that I had my second brush with the Devil. Since my conversion I had not met a single Christian with a background like mine. Certainly the members of St Anselm's were respectable to the core, baptised at birth, confirmed at eleven, and sitting in the pew on Sunday in the manner to which they had been accustomed all their lives. Even the more active believers I came across in rehabilitation work were from quiet, ordinary homes. They knew about the spiritist churches, but they had never been inside one, and had certainly not been possessed by evil spirits. This rather unenviable distinction I had all to myself; as a result I was forced to conclude that the Devil played no part in the everyday life of a Christian and that as far as I was concerned he might just as well *not* exist anymore.

I was happy enough to believe it! My only regrets were that so few people seemed to understand my story. At the same time I was learning fast about the power of prayer. One drug addict at Portal House had recently agreed to go 'cold turkey' – that is, stop his heroin intake abruptly with no chemical substitutes – provided that Tom would pray for him. In consequence he did not suffer a single symptom of withdrawal. That really stunned me, because I'd seen other addicts try the same thing without prayer and go through days of the most awful pain. What impressed me most was that Tom expected it to happen. There was no fuss made over it; he just prayed, and then – a miracle took place. It had never struck me before that miracles were meant to be part of the everyday experience of the believer.

Not long after that incident I spent part of a Saturday afternoon cleaning the car. The Consul had been sold some time ago and I'd replaced it with a black Austin Cambridge. It was midsummer, one of those hot, close days that are ideal for doing an outside job. I filled a bucket with soapy water, threw in a sponge, and rolling my sleeves up went out into the front garden.

Everything went well for the first ten minutes. Then I discovered that a mark I'd been rubbing furiously was in fact on the inside of the window, and I crawled on to the back seat to get at it. The seat was burning hot in the sunshine and because I flinched as I climbed in I somehow managed to slam the door behind me. I sighed, and set to work on the stain. It soon came off, and I wriggled round to get out — only to find the door wouldn't open. I pushed and rattled it for quite a while before I realised what was wrong.

The Austin Cambridge had a child-proof lock on the rear doors. This creditable device was meant to prevent small children opening the door while the car was in motion. Having no small children I had never had occasion to use it, and had consequently forgotten it was there. Getting in to wash the window, though, I must have accidently pushed the lever up and so activated the lock. It was now impossible to open the door from the inside.

This might have proved a serious problem had I not left the other three doors wide open. I clambered across the seat to get out and stood for a moment on the drive, mopping my brow. For some reason I couldn't identify, that child-proof lock struck me as important. It was almost as if God was telling me to remember it, though it seemed to me peculiar to be putting it in those terms. I hadn't had much experience of receiving instructions from God — or from anyone else on the other side — since my days in spiritism. And this feeling was vastly different from being bawled at by the Guide. I dismissed the thought from my mind and got back to work.

That night I was on duty at the Samaritans. I arrived at the Romford office at eight, and checked who was on staff for the evening. Two people were on — a young couple called Brenda and Ian. We started off chatting to an old man with a drink problem. He was a regular both with us and the pub down the road. He often dropped in for a cup of tea, swearing that drink would be the death of him and as from that night he was going to give it up. He never did. When the first telephone call came in I retired to the back room to take it. There were three more calls, one a potential suicide, and that kept me busy for most of the evening.

At about ten I heard a loud wailing out in the front office. I finished the call and went out to see what was going on. Sitting on the rather threadbare sofa was a woman of about forty, her face buried in a handkerchief, weeping uncontrollably. She had jet-black, curly hair and, to judge by the colour of the handkerchief, was heavily made up. An assortment of copper bracelets jangled on her left wrist.

'What's the problem?' I said to Ian.

'We can't tell.'

Brenda was sitting beside the woman with an arm round her shoulder. 'She says she can't face going home on the train.'

'Where does she live?'

'Luton. She's been here with relatives. She's got a return ticket but she's frightened to use it.'

'Did she give you her name?'

'Alice.'

I knelt down in front of the woman. 'Alice, you don't need to cry. You're with friends here.'

She cried even more loudly.

'Can't you tell us what's the matter?'

But nothing I said got the slightest response. At length Ian said, 'It's getting on for ten-thirty. Brenda and I have got to leave soon.'

'And the office closes at eleven. We can't leave her here all night.'

There was a pause.

'Perhaps we should just drop her at the station on our way back, and hope for the best?' said Brenda.

I nodded. 'That's awfully kind of you. I really don't see any alternative.'

They got her to her feet and walked slowly out of the door, one on either side, Brenda holding Alice's shiny, black handbag. I saw them out, then sat down in front of the telephone. No one rang. At ten forty-five they were back again.

'She got as far as the barrier, then she collapsed,' said Ian. 'So we had to bring her back.'

He was breathing hard. I could see that both of them wanted to get away, so I said, 'Don't worry, leave her with me. I'll think of something to do, even if it's only calling the ambulance.'

They offered to stay on, but I refused. When they'd gone I drew up a chair and sat facing Alice, who was still crying, her handkerchief now screwed up into a little ball. I felt sorry for her. There was evidently something worrying her so much that she couldn't even express it. I thought about the drug addict I'd seen taken off heroin a few days before, and an idea came to me. Why not pray for her? True, it was against the rules of the Samaritans to impose any personal religious views on a client; but there was no one else here, and surely, in a case of such extreme distress ...

She was shaking her head now and wailing, 'No one can help me. No one!'

I plucked up courage. 'I know someone who can help you, Alice,' I said. 'The Lord Jesus.'

She changed in an instant. Suddenly the lean, quaking figure sat up rigid, fists clenched in her lap. For the first time I saw her face straight on; it was set hard and deeply lined, a dark tropical tint to the skin. Her eyes, still red with tears, blazed at me angrily.

'Don't use that name in front of me,' she said with slow venom. 'My parents promised me to the Devil, and I belong to him!'

On reflex I had half risen from my seat. I stayed still, watching to see what she would do. She didn't move, and soon I saw that her eyes, though wide open, had lost their animation. She seemed to have had some sort of seizure and lost consciousness. Gradually she subsided and slumped forward on to the floor, upsetting as she did so the teacup on the arm of the sofa.

I became aware that I was breathing again. Rubbing my hands together I found them moist with perspiration. It was a long time since I'd met someone who talked about the Devil, and I wasn't enjoying the introduction: the memories stirred by the name were too painful for me. I stood at a distance looking at the body, letting my thoughts settle again like a fine sediment in the lower reaches of the mind.

Was she to be taken seriously? Possession by evil spirits seemed to me such a rare phenomenon that on reflection I was disinclined to believe her. Schizophrenics also talked about the Devil on occasions, without ever having been possessed. A mental condition like that would surely explain her sudden, irrational fear of travelling home on the train. At any rate, something had to be done, and pretty smartly: I had to close the office in fifteen minutes.

After a moment's deliberation I hit on a plan. Since Alice was afraid to return home by train and, anyway, appeared to be out for the count, I would simply haul her into the car and take her to Luton myself. It was Sunday tomorrow and I could sleep in before church. That way at least the problem would be dealt with and she would be off my hands. I cleared up the broken remains of the teacup, then went round the building turning out the lights.

I was just on the point of tackling Alice when the phone rang. It was Tom Marriott.

'Glad I caught you, Robert. I don't know why, but I've really had it on my mind to pray for you all day.'

I laughed. 'I could do with a bit of prayer right now, Tom. We've had a woman here who says her parents promised her to the Devil. She came in crying because she couldn't face a journey back to Luton.'

'Where is she now?' said Tom. There was a hint of urgency in his voice.

'Well, here. Stretched out on the floor, actually. I was just about to load her into the car and take her back myself.'

'Don't.'

'It's OK, Tom, I can handle it. Really I can.'

'Don't, for heaven's sake. It's too dangerous.'

I rolled my eyes. 'Well, what am I meant to do with her, then?'

Tom paused. 'Hang on there,' he said. 'I'll be round in a jiffy and go along with you.'

He hung up. I replaced the phone and leaned against the desk with my arms folded. Alice was still lying prone in the middle of the room. It wouldn't take Tom long to arrive — his house was only just round the corner from the office. He soon came, but not alone. He had brought a friend, a voluntary helper at Portal House, who was going to travel part of the way with us.

'OK,' said Tom, when he saw Alice, 'let's get her outside. Get on the other side of her, Mike.'

Taking one arm each they picked her up and started to drag her through the door. I locked up behind them then ran ahead to let them into the car. It was warm and humid outside. Though it had been a clear day no stars were visible overhead. In the distance I thought I heard the roll of thunder.

Alice had come round and was struggling feebly.

'Come on, dear, no need to make a fuss,' said Tom. 'We're just going to take you back home. Good, that's it, nice and easy ...'

'No. No!' she moaned.

'Try and get her other arm round, Mike.'

'No! I won't go anywhere with Jesus. I belong to the Devil!'

She was starting to put up quite a fight. At last we managed to wrestle her into the rear seat, Tom sitting on her right, Mike in the passenger seat next to me. I turned the ignition and revved.

'Let me go!' snarled Alice. 'If you don't let me go I'll wait till we're on the motorway then I'll throw myself out. Try explaining *that* to the police.'

It was then that I remembered the child-proof locks. I leaned round, released and pushed open the back door on Alice's side, engaged the lock, and pulled it closed. Whatever else she did, she wouldn't be able to jump out. We were off.

Mike lived about a mile down the London Road. Alice kicked and complained all the way. I felt her foot thudding into my seat on more than one occasion, but somehow Tom managed to hold her down and we arrived at Mike's flat. He climbed out. 'I'll be praying,' he said. 'That woman is full of evil spirits. Don't take any chances with her.'

'Ought we to go at all?' I said, looking round nervously.

'We've come this far,' said Tom, 'so we might as well go on. Just watch out. Mike's right. She's possessed, and that means the Devil is likely to attack us.'

'Attack us?' I was appalled. I had images of being flipped sideways into the gutter by a red, clawed finger.

'Keep on praying, we'll be all right. Jesus has the victory over Satan.'

We set off again, working our way round the north side of London towards the M 10. The thunder was coming closer, and we were seeing the first big splashes of rain on the windscreen. The onset of the storm seemed to make Alice even more agitated. She cried out and squirmed with every flicker of lightning. Suddenly the fields around us lit up as if under a gigantic flashbulb, and the rain fell in a torrent. I slowed down, peering over the wheel to make out the road ahead. It was fading quickly under the constant slurry of water on the windscreen. The wipers did nothing but sweep the flow from side to side as it came down. At last, in desperation, I rolled down the window and found my way over to the kerb. We took it with a bump.

'Let's get this straight, Tom. Do we go on or not? If we go much further we're going to drown.'

'The rain'll ease off.'

'Can't we just drop her at a police station or something?'

For a moment Tom didn't reply; he was praying. 'No,' he said at last, 'Jesus is stronger than anything the Devil can throw at us. We're going on.'

'Satan!' hissed Alice. 'Where are you, Satan?'

Her voice was eerie, separated as we were from the rest of the world by a torrential fall of rain. I shivered, even though I was warm.

'Alice,' said Tom, 'Listen to me. Just because your parents promised you to the Devil doesn't mean you're under his power. You can be set free.'

'Satan! Satan!'

'Satan's pulling the wool over your eyes, Alice. You don't want to belong to him. Trust in Jesus.'

I heard Alice convulse. I was under no illusions now – she was as much possessed as I had been. I felt sorry for her. But it was fast becoming clear that her case was far worse than mine. I had wanted to find help: Alice was running from it.

Tom was trying to keep hold of her and draw her out of the hallucination. 'Alice,' he said, clearly and steadily, 'I'm going to pray for you. Listen, if you can, and pray along with me.'

'I'll scream if you start praying,' snapped Alice.

'OK, then I'll pray quietly.'

There was a deafening shriek, louder even than the persistent peals of thunder. Alice was struggling and screaming and calling out to the Devil.

'You all right, Tom?'

'Just about. Let's get moving again. I want to be out of this as soon as possible.'

Fortunately the rain was letting up a bit. I pulled out on to the road again and accelerated to around fifty-five. Soon we had hit the motorway and were speeding towards the M 1 junction south of St Albans. I heard Tom's voice from the rear.

'I've never felt evil like this, Robert. It's getting worse.'

'Can you hold on?' I said.

'How far now?'

'About – ' I stopped short. In the far distance I could see a man, standing at the roadside with his arm raised. At first I thought he was a hitch-hiker, but any hitch-hiker out in a storm like this must have needed his head examined. We sped closer. At about two hundred yards I realised this was no ordinary man, and my heart started to race. He wore a white robe that glistened under the headlamps, an obscure symbol blazoned on his chest.

'Tom!'

Alice suddenly wrenched herself free of Tom's grasp and lunged against the door. Before he could restrain her she had her hands on the handle and was shaking it frantically. I glanced round in alarm — then remembered the locks.

'It's OK, Tom. She can't get out.'

I looked back immediately to locate the man in white — but he was gone. Had we passed him? I slowed down, searching the mirror. Behind me the rear window was as blank as a dead television screen. It was possible that the darkness had simply swallowed him up, or that he had hidden himself by crouching down off the road. But my instincts told me otherwise.

Alice was now screaming hysterically, beating her fists against the door. 'Kill them, Satan!' she shrieked. 'Kill them! Kill them!'

Nothing Tom could do held her down. It was at that point that my nerves started to fail me. I fully expected to be grabbled at any minute from behind and strangled to death. I looked firmly out in front and began to recite the Lord's Prayer, loudly, over and over.

Alice went on screaming until sheer exhaustion reduced her to silence. After that she simply panted, her breath rasping in and out as if she were in the last throes of respiratory illness. In the end she melted into tears, and sat sobbing on Tom's shoulder for the rest of the journey. The anger of the evil spirits within her, like the storm, had died down and left her quiet again. But I didn't relax. I had reached 'For thine is the kingdom' thirty times before we drove into Luton.

We drew up at the address that Alice, between sobs, had told us was her home. Tom and I exchanged glances, then I got out and helped him lift Alice from the car. We went with her to the door. I knew what was on Tom's mind.

'You're feeling better, aren't you?' he said, gently.

She nodded.

'The Devil's been giving you a rough time. That was quite a fit you threw while we were coming.'

She brushed her hair back, not meeting Tom's eyes. 'Yes, I'm sorry. Thank you for bringing me.' She fumbled for her key.

'Alice,' Tom was urgent. 'You can think for yourself again now. You know what the Devil is doing to you; you've seen the power of Jesus protecting us on our journey through that storm. He can change your life as easily as he changes the weather. He can release you. You only have to ask ... '

There was a tantalizing pause. Alice was looking, abstracted, into the night. Dimly, I remembered the time when I had stood in the hall at *Pendragon,* torn between going on up to the familiar suffering in my room and going back, pursuing the last chance of freedom. Suddenly Alice thrust the key in and turned it. 'No. No, I can't. It's just impossible – no one can help me now.' She gave a brief smile. 'Goodnight.'

And that was it.

I remember that a sense of deep sadness came over us. It was the more poignant for me because I might so easily have gone the same way as Alice and rejected the help that Jesus offered. There was nothing for us to do but leave her. She clearly had no wish to be persuaded, and prayers for deliverance would be without effect if she didn't want to be set free. We could only pray that one day she would. Until that time, I knew only too well what she would be going through.

I never met Alice again, but as I moved into the orbit of St Paul's in Hainault I came across scores of people with the same sort of problem. Some were hard and cynical and like Alice eventually slipped back into the Devil's grasp; others pulled through. But they kept on coming, like a stream of refugees from a war-zone, miserable, their lives broken. And they are still coming. They are the living evidence of the Devil's brutal activities in modern twentieth century life.

Society, of course, dismisses them as mental cases or nervous breakdowns. That is to be expected – a world that considers the Devil to be a myth will hardly give any credence to stories about witches, spells and demons. But here is a paradox: on the one hand the world around us condemns belief in the Devil as so much Medieval nonsense; on the other, it takes a morbid interest in the trappings of devilry – the success of recent occult horror movies is proof enough of that. Why this contradiction? The answer, I am sure, goes back to the Devil himself. Scepticism about the occult suits him very well – it is a perfect cover beneath which to promote evil and suffering in the human race. But he is never beyond reach to those who really want to find him. I know that from personal experience. Dotted across the surface of this humdrum life we lead are spiritual quicksands to which most people are completely blind.

It is one of the purposes of this book to heal that blindness, to counter the overwhelming modern ignorance about the Devil and his work. So in the last chapters I want to ask again the question that a long time ago I asked of Mr Hartley:

Who is the Devil?

9: Who is the Devil?

This question has been answered in a bewildering variety of ways. Many will say flatly that he doesn't exist, that he is a figment of the imagination. Others, mindful of the world's troubles, will declare him to be the personification of evil, an example of man's persistent habit of putting faces to things that are really abstract. A third group will admit he exists, but add that traditional religion has misrepresented him. He is, they will say, a being who encourages man towards individuality and self-realisation. Finally there are people like my grandmother, for whom the Devil is a goat-footed creature with horns and a trident who tempts overweight ladies into eating a fifth jam doughnut!

As it happens, none of these answers is correct. But how can we be sure? After all, it is very unpopular today to insist that one religious view is right and all the others wrong. If we are going to say that the Devil really exists we must have some good reason for saying it. Nor is it good enough to base our case on personal experience. As you will know by now I have a very clear idea what the Devil is like — I've met him! But that in itself doesn't oblige anyone else to believe my story. We need to refer to some reliable authority on the matter which will tell us categorically who the Devil is. And the best authority on the Devil is the book that first mentioned him — the Bible.

The Bible is probably the most widely read, and the most poorly understood book the world has ever known. Certainly when I was a teenager the most recent available translation was the Authorised Version of 1611 — already 400 years old. No wonder I found it hard to read! Today, though, there are many modern translations, and anyone can read the Bible in simple, everyday English.

Nevertheless it remains very hard to decide 'what the Bible says' over all, just by a cursory reading. There are many reasons for this. Not least is that the Bible is not a single book. It is actually a collection of books, written over a period of some thousand years between about 1000 BC and the time of Christ, bound together in the same set of covers. The sorts of writing included in these sixty-six books are diverse: there are histories, biographies, love poetry, prophecies, letters and short stories, not to mention the four Gospels and the dazzling visions of Revelation, which seem to belong in classes of their own.

Finding the common thread in all these types of literature can be confusing. But a couple of simple guidelines help a lot. The Bible as a whole can be seen as God's message to man, given through a number of different authors, and telling us what God, the real Author, is like. Most of what we call the Old Testament concerns God's dealings with the Israelites (from whom the modern Jews are descended). This nation God chose as his representatives in a world that had grown estranged from him. By and large they did the job rather poorly, and as their failures mount up in the pages of the Old Testament we detect a new strand, the promise that one day God himself will visit the earth and set it to rights. This he did in the person of Jesus Christ, who was at the same time the supreme Jew, the supreme man, and the supreme God. The life of Jesus, and some letters written by his early followers, are recorded in the second and shorter part of the Bible called the New Testament. What God's visit means we shall see later on.

The Devil is mentioned several times in the Bible, most often in the later books. No writer describes him at any length, and the information we are given comes in a series of glimpses which have to be pieced together if we are to build up a picture of his character and work. It is an intriguing investigation. We can begin with a remark made by Jesus that is recorded in the Gospel of Luke. He had sent out some of his followers and given them authority to deliver people from evil spirits, just as the ministers at Watford delivered me. These followers returned, evidently very struck by the novelty of their experience. It was then that Jesus told them: 'I saw Satan fall like lightning from heaven'

(Luke 10.18).

What did he mean? One thing we can deduce from this verse is that Jesus was no ordinary human being. The event he saw occurred in the supernatural world outside the space and time of our own universe, and was of cosmic significance. We find what is probably another reference to it in the last book of the Bible, Revelation, which is a series of visions given to a man called John, an early follower of Jesus who for his faith had been imprisoned on the lonely Mediterranean Island of Patmos:

> Now war arose in heaven, Michael and his angels
> fighting against the dragon; and the dragon and his
> angels fought, but they were defeated and there was no
> longer any place for them in heaven. And the great
> dragon was thrown down, that ancient serpent, who is
> called the Devil and Satan, the deceiver of the whole
> world – he was thrown down to the earth, and his
> angels were thrown down with him (Rev.12.7-9).

John saw in this vision one set of angels fighting against another. An angel is a spiritual being, and God created many of them before he created the earth and mankind. We are used to thinking of angels as big, effeminate choirboys with wings and haloes, but this idea, like the Devil's horn, is not found in the Bible and has no foundation in fact. Nor is it true, as we see here, that all angels are good. In this passage a whole host of angels are evil and under the leadership of the Devil, who is described very picturesquely as a dragon and a serpent. It was in this battle that the rebellious force fell 'like lightning from heaven', overcome by the faithful angels of God.

But John says quite clearly that the Devil and his angels once occupied a place in heaven. It is unlikely that good and evil would be found so close together, especially in the presence of God himself; so we may presume that at some time in the mists of the distant past the Devil himself was good. How could God have created him otherwise? That means that at some stage an awful tragedy occurred, that a great and good angel stooped to rebellion, and drew a large part of the angelic force with him. In other words, there was an attempted *coup* in heaven.

The cause of this disaster we can only guess at. It is worth quoting, though, a passage from the Old Testament that many feel throws light on the problem. The passage was written by a prophet – a special messenger of God – called Isaiah, in the seventh century BC. Around that time Israel was overrun by a fierce foreign power known as Babylon. Militarily, Babylon was as good as invincible, but the prophet looked forward to a time when God would punish it for its cruelty. He penned the following angry verses:

How you are fallen from heaven,
  O Day Star, Son of Dawn!
How you are cut down to the ground,
  you who laid the nations low!
You said in your heart,
  'I will ascend to heaven;
above the stars of God
  I will set my throne on high;
I will sit on the mount of assembly in the far north;
I will ascend above the heights of the clouds,
  I will make myself like the Most High.'
But you are brought down to Sheol,
  to the depths of the Pit (Isa.14.12-15).

The immediate point is obvious. Isaiah means to show that Babylon has overreached itself, that its kings have thought themselves so powerful that they could displace God himself. It is a hollow conceit; time alone will see their empire crumble and its mighty men descend to Sheol, the place of the dead. That is perhaps as much as we are intended to find in the passage. At the same time the ambition of the Babylonians is a vain one for mere mortal men, and some scholars have suggested that the pride of Babylon is a reflection of a far greater pride – the Devil's. The kings of Babylon might have aimed, figuratively, to make themselves like the Most High. But the Devil could have thought himself really capable of such a feat. This idea is at least probable, and has gained enough support for the name Day Star in this passage to have been given to the Devil in its Latin form, Lucifer.

Whatever the cause of the rebellion, it is certain that it happened, and that, as a result, the Devil and his angels were driven out. Since then, he has been the sworn enemy of God, and has attempted to destroy God's work in whatever way he can. It is for this he has earned the Hebrew name Satan, which means simply, 'adversary'. He is the enemy of God and because man is the creation of God, he is man's enemy, too. In fact the Devil's ejection from heaven was an ill omen for the earth. The vision of John quoted earlier from the book of Revelation finishes like this:

> And I heard a loud voice in heaven, saying ...
> 'Rejoice then, O heaven and you that dwell therein! But woe to you, O earth and sea, for the devil has come down to you in great wrath, because he knows that his time is short!' (Rev.12.10,12).

The Devil has been thrown out of heaven and is biding his time down here on the earth until he is finally captured and punished. The 'short' time, of course, should be understood in cosmic terms: the whole history of the world is a fleeting moment in the context of God's eternity. The final overthrow of Satan, and the events that immediately precede it, are also recorded in the visions of Revelation, and make grim reading. But that time is yet to come. For the moment the Devil and his angels are with us on the earth – to be more accurate, with us in the universe – and are angrily making havoc of God's creation. In a very real sense the Devil controls events in human history, for Jesus describes him as the 'ruler of this world' (John 14.30). It should therefore not surprise us that the world has from its earliest times been full of cruelty and unhappiness; we know who is behind the scenes and pulling a lot of the important strings.

Satan established his control over the world of human affairs at a very early stage. The story is recorded for us in the opening chapters of the Bible, in the book of Genesis. After creating the world, God entrusted his special creation, man, with the job of looking after it. Adam, in fact, is the Hebrew word for man; Eve is derived from the word for mother. So besides being the first parents of the human race Adam and Eve also represent it.

God put them in a perfect paradise called Eden, where hardship and sorrow were unknown. But among the privileges he gave them to enjoy was a single prohibition: they were not to eat the fruit of the tree in the middle of the garden, the tree of the knowledge of good and evil, because to eat of that tree would bring certain death.

Well, we all know what happened. The serpent came along and persuaded Eve to eat the fruit of the tree, and after she'd taken a bite she thought it was good, so she gave some to Adam as well. But notice a couple of things about the story. One, that it was the serpent that tempted Eve. It is no coincidence that John refers to Satan as the ancient serpent in Revelation; the snake in Eden was none other than the Devil himself in disguise. Two, note how he went about persuading her. He told Eve that if she disobeyed God, and ate of the fruit of the tree, she would become like God. Once again, is it a coincidence that this very same ambition was the one present in Satan's heart when he rebelled against the Most High in heaven? Probably not. The Devil was trying to press mankind into his own mould – that of the rebel against God. And what's more, he succeeded.

By disobeying God – the God who had freely given them everything they enjoyed and had laid on them only one command – Adam and Eve fell, as in the misty past before them the Devil had fallen. They were driven out of Eden. The rebellion had taken root in them, and it was there to stay. There is not a single human being who is not in essence a rebel against his creator. All of us have that fatal inclination to please ourselves before we please God, and thus it is impossible for us to enjoy the free relationship with God that Adam and Eve once had, and which we were all intended to share.

This poison with which the Devil injected the first man and woman was quick to spread. We read in the fourth chapter of Genesis that an argument between two of their sons resulted in the world's first homicide. The disharmony between man and God naturally produced disharmony between man and man. That is the poison that has been passed down through every race and generation. Often our nerves are dulled to it; we are so used to seeing violence on the television that events in the Middle East and Northern Ireland fail to horrify us as they should. And yet the same poison is at work in our own society, on our own streets, in our own minds. We can't shut it out because it lives inside us. Every mean and petty thought expresses and reinforces the rebellion that runs in our veins. And it is this — all that is worst, most sick and evil in human nature — that characterises the Devil. 'Rebel' is a vogue term today; it conjures romantic notions of freedom fighters like Che Guevara. But the first rebel, Satan, would sicken you too much to have his face stamped on your tee-shirt. All that is vile and vicious and warped and diseased has its root in the Devil. He is all of these qualities in their most extreme form: the absolute opposite of God.

Having administered the poison, however, he has retreated behind the scenes. What we see in the world today is not the Devil in person, but the evidence of his work. There is a good reason for this. It seems that in the early history of the human race the material and spiritual worlds were to some extent blended together. Now they have drifted apart; the supernatural has receded into a sort of mist, and because few have any direct experience of it (especially in our own Western society) it is generally ignored. We no longer expect to see angels or talking serpents. Our world is one of material objects, of human action, personality and history. True, some people claim to have penetrated the mist and contacted the supernatural; but they can't *prove* its existence, and so few people believe them. We take seriously only what we can detect with our senses, and because the supernatural cannot generally be experienced in this way, we suppose that it doesn't exist.

This was much the sort of position I reached at the end of Mr Hartley's confirmation class. Being unable to see God and the Devil, I concluded they weren't there. It was only after investigating spiritism that I changed my mind. You see, spiritists lay great emphasis on *demonstrating* the supernatural, and so 'proving' it to exist. That is the reason for the 'proofs of survival' that play such a key role in their meetings. They may not be able to prove by logic that the supernatural exists, but they try, as it were, to take journeys into the mist to find it, and so experience it first-hand.

That was enough to convince me. The supernatural world was as real to me then as the lunar dust must have been to Armstrong when he first set foot on the moon. I knew it through personal encounter. But here we come to a crucial problem. You see, it is one thing to demonstrate that the supernatural world is there, but quite another to find out what sort of place it is. I know, for instance, that Antarctica exists, but I certainly wouldn't want to live there. And if I'd known twenty-four years ago what the supernatural world was like I wouldn't have begun my fateful journey into it.

Of the dangers that lay ahead of me the spiritists gave me not one word of warning. It is possible they were unaware of them. They were like old boy scouts urging me to go hiking in Central America, telling me about all the beautiful and interesting scenery and forgetting to mention that a guerrilla war was in progress. For that is just about the size of things in the supernatural world. The spiritists might tell us their tales about the peace and happiness of departed souls, the paradise they live in and the love that is found between them. But the cold fact is there's a war going on.

That is one of the main points I want to get across in writing this book. The supernatural world is not a safe place: it is a war zone. It has been a war zone since the Devil's first revolt and his fall, like lightning, from heaven. And it is impossible to enter the supernatural realm without finding yourself on one side or the other – on God's side or the Devil's. There is no such thing as an impartial observer of the supernatural. In the end there is no means of investigating it, in the way I tried to do, from a detached, scientific standpoint. To investigate it is to be involved, just as surely as you cannot experience life without belonging to a particular race.

Spiritism is one example. If you go into spiritism you will certainly find yourself draughted, just as I was, into the Devil's forces. The organisation is just a front, a glossy exterior to lure the victim in. I don't mean that many spiritists aren't sincere in their beliefs or that attending seances immediately makes them evil or unpleasant in their behaviour. Many of the spiritists I met were decent, ordinary people. But they were deceived; they didn't know who was using them, and to what purpose.

This goes for a vast number of religions and practices. Like spiritism, they draw the inquirer into closer contact with the Devil. Some are serious, some seem trivial; some are full-blown systems of belief, others are almost unconscious habits. But all of them have the same effect: they emphasise rebellion against God and bring the person who practises them into line with the Devil's forces. It is common today to speak of countries being 'aligned' with the West or with the Soviet bloc. Well, the same is true in the supernatural world. You are aligned to God's side or to Satan's. Tampering with the supernatural will only confirm your alignment to the Devil.

What sort of activities have this effect? There are many of them – more than I can explain or even mention here. But they fall into four distinct groups. Each group combines activities that are broadly similar in purpose, and although the purpose differs between one group and the next all four converge like roads on the same place. Remember them.

The first group approaches the supernatural world with a view to *obtaining information*. Much of what is now called spiritism comes into this category. Spiritism underwent a revival in nineteenth-century America, but in fact it had been known since antiquity. Its proper name is *Necromancy*, meaning simply 'the calling of the dead'. Spirits of deceased people are contacted with a ouija board or through a medium and asked for information about the afterlife or the future. As I myself discovered, some very convincing 'confirmations' are given. But I doubt now whether the spirit that called itself Meg was really that of my mother. The Bible indicates that the dead go to Hades or paradise (according to the quality of their earthly life) and that these are places of waiting from which, except under very special circumstances, they cannot be recalled. If this is so we may conclude that the spiritual forces present at a seance are a good deal less harmless than the spiritists suppose.

Spiritism has a following of millions, particularly in developing countries such as those in South America, but it is not as common as many other beliefs of the same type. Most widespread, perhaps is *Superstition*. Few people have not at some time in their lives hoped for 'good luck' when going on a journey or making a bet. It is a way of coming to terms with situations they cannot control. The gambler will often trust his luck when the statistical odds are loaded heavily against him – and fortunately for the betting shops his luck usually lets him down! But superstition affects people who have never risked their money on anything more dangerous than a building society. Its forms are almost innumerable. We all know the example of the superstitious man who, on going to work one day, is delighted to see a black cat cross his path. This is a sign that good luck will follow. Unfortunately, though, the cat then changes its mind and crosses back the other way, thus turning the good luck to bad. Being a cautious type, the man decides he had better return home to prevent any further mishaps. But entering his living-room he flings open a window and inadvertently lets in a sparrow. This is bad news, because a bird in the house forebodes the death of one of the occupants. Could it be him? Anxious, he examines his face in the mirror for any symptoms of disease. He finds none, but in his nervousness knocks the mirror down and breaks it. He has hit the jackpot. Now his bad luck will last, with no possible remedy, for seven years ...

People like this are easy to make fun of, yet they are really only trying to make their future secure. All of us sense that the universe is a potentially hostile place, and while we hope that the future will bring us pleasure and success we suspect there are some nasty surprises in store. Worse still, our fate seems to be decided at random. We are happy to have Ernie pick our number on the Premium Bonds, but what about that other 'Ernie' who may select us for unemployment or multiple sclerosis?

It is in the face of these uncertainties that we seek reassurance about what is to come. Why, then, should a belief in luck bring us into line with the Devil? The answer is found in the principle of trust. The Bible states categorically that the future lies in God's hands, and his alone. We are told to put our trust in him as a faithful friend who will guide us through all the joys and hardships of life. But superstition makes this impossible.

Let's go back to our superstitious friend to see why. This man pays attention to certain signs that will, he thinks, give information on his prospects. Discovering an open safety pin, for instance, he will brace himself for some bad luck. He may feel it is in the nature of the universe that open safety pins should have this effect, or he may feel that there is a god somewhere who impartially deals out good and back luck according to the dictates of the signs. In neither case is he trusting the God the Bible speaks of. There is no concept of 'luck' in Christianity; future well-being, in so far as it depends on the individual at all, depends on his obedience to God's commands, and assurance comes not through any petty signs but a sure trust in the care of a loving Creator. To take superstition seriously is thus an implicit rejection of God.

Of course, there is only one person who stands to gain by this: the Devil. Not only will our friend make life a misery for himself by anticipating disasters that are never going to happen, he will be playing into the hands of the rebellious angels. They are quite capable of influencing events in a man's life just enough to persuade him that his 'luck' really works. In that way they cause him to stray from a trusting relationship with God into the territory of the Devil.

Exactly the same may be said of several other practices. *Astrology*, which originated in the ancient civilisations of the Middle East, and gained a foothold in France during the sixteenth century (when the French king kept an astrologer at court), has in our own time become extremely popular. It claims that a person's destiny and character will be determined by the position of the stars and constellations at the time of his birth. These positions may be discerned by casting a *Horoscope*, which will reveal the sign of the *Zodiac* under which he was born. Many magazines and newspapers now carry horoscopes, giving predictions for people born under all twelve signs. For those who favour long-term forecasts, astrological calendars, or *Almanacs*, are available. Many astrologers will say that their practice is scientific, but this is manifestly untrue. It has no more basis in science than superstition does.

Several other activities fulfil a similar function. *Palmistry*, a common entertainment at funfairs, foretells the future not by consulting the stars, but by examining the lines on a person's palm. *Crystal balls* and *tea leaves* are used in a similar way, and even handwriting can be analysed for what it tells about the writer's character or fortune. Other variations include the use of the *pendulum*, which can, among other things, find lost objects and determine the sex of eggs, and *water divining* – the use of hazel twigs, whale bone or forked wire to locate underground water, on the assumption that all objects emit 'radiations' which, if they are of a certain type, will cause the divining rod to turn.

So far as the spiritual war is concerned all these practices are on a par with superstition. They seek information or reassurance from a source other than God, and thus have one foot planted firmly in the Devil's camp. Of course, you may think that no one takes them seriously, especially the crystal balls and tea leaves. But many do; and others, who have no conscious religious beliefs, are superstitious by habit. Even sceptics have the occasional doubt, because in the end they can't be sure whether there's anything in it or not. Put yourself to the test: could you just laugh it off if a fortune-teller informed you that in three years' time you were going to die of cancer?

If you did take such a prediction seriously, you would be strongly motivated to do something about it. And that brings us to the second group of practices – those by which it is possible to *manipulate the future*. Superstition, of course, lends itself to this purpose very easily. Some actions are thought to induce good luck, such as wearing a shark's tooth, saying 'touch wood' when speaking of illness, putting a horseshoe over a door, keeping your fingers crossed. Others provide remedies for sickness, some of them very bizarre.

A woman who wears stockings, for instance, may cure a sore throat by tying the left stocking round her neck. A less appetising treatment, this time for warts, involves rubbing the affected part with a black snail which is afterwards to be impaled on a thorn of the same colour. As the snail dries out and shrivels, so, it is said, will the wart!

These kind of remedies, especially the ones involving special prayers, holy oil or water, and invocations of the Trinity, are often referred to as *white magic*. Those who practise it are careful to distinguish it from *black magic*, which differs, they say, in that its purposes are evil and not good. From the biblical standpoint the distinction is meaningless. Both varieties derive their power from a source other than the Christian God, and if in white magic the nature of that source is sometimes obscure, in black magic it emerges very clearly as Satanic.

We are not talking here about the sort of magic that conjurers perform on television: that is a very deft skill in creating optical illusions which is usually harmless. Magic in the religious sense has its roots in ancient civilisations as diverse as the Chinese and the Persian. Like spiritism it has undergone a dramatic revival in the last century. Significantly, it is the blacker side of the cult – that devoted to decidedly sinister purposes – that has proved most successful. The casting of spells isn't restricted to fairy-tales: it really happens, and it's effective. Covens are springing up all over the British Isles, and young people particularly are being drawn into them. Many witches are quite frank about the fact that they are in the service of Satan, and it is hardly surprising that all witchcraft and magic is strongly opposed to Christianity. It is here that the hidden spiritual war begins to surface.

Other practices allow the manipulation of future events without appealing quite so crudely as magic does to the individual's lust for power. Many offer healing, among them spiritism as I encountered it at Amersham Place. The effect that it had on me is, I think, enough to show that this sort of healing is less than beneficial. But almost everyone falls ill at some time in his life, and for this reason the attraction of practices offering healing is very strong. Others that specialise in it include *Christian Science* (which, it has been aptly said, is neither Christian nor scientific), and the *Aetherius Society,* another system that claims to use spiritual radiations. The same goes for all of them: they derive their power from a source other than the true God, and so even if the miracles they perform are authentic (which they sometimes are) they are gateways to the realm of the Devil.

Of course the gateways rarely have signs over them to tell us where they lead. No military leader in a war will want it known where all his troops are stationed, least of all the Devil. But it is clear with many of the beliefs we are talking about that they have clear religious overtones. Many of them contain an explicitly supernatural element that encourages the newcomer to enter them as a devotee, or in plain language, as a worshipper. At first sight this might seem presumptuous and rather off-putting. But it must be remembered that some of these beliefs have the advantage of being (or seeming) new, and that they provide an alternative to the Christianity that many people, especially young people, feel is worn out and dull.

These so-called *'new religions'* form the third approach to the supernatural. Many of the most recent ones have come from the Orient and were popularised in the West during the 1960s by groups like the Beatles. Examples are *Transcendental Meditation,* the *Divine Light Mission, Hare Krishna, Baha'ism,* and the *Unification Church of Sun Myung Moon.* But these were by no means the first; *Theosophy, Mormonism* and *Seventh Day Adventism* date from the nineteenth century, while *Sweden-borgianism* (a sort of spiritism) goes back to the eighteenth, and *Rosicrucianism* to the Middle Ages.

They are very diverse in their beliefs and practices. The *Jehovah's Witnesses*, for example, share with Christians a great respect for the Bible, but interpret it on radically different lines (so different, in fact, that they have found it necessary to 'retranslate' it). Theosophy, at the other extreme, has a teaching of self-knowledge much like that of Hinduism, and lays no claim to be rooted in the Christian tradition. The details are too many and complex to go into here, but we should take note of some of the things the Bible has to say about them. From the viewpoint of the biblical authors they can be summed up in a single word: idolatry. That means the pursuit of idols, or false gods. The judgment on them is emphatic:

> Those who lavish gold from the purse,
>   and weigh out silver in the scales,
> hire a goldsmith, and he makes it into a god;
>   then they fall down and worship!
> They lift it upon their shoulders, they carry it,
>   they set it in its place, and it stands there;
>   it cannot move from its place.
> If one cries to it, it does not answer
>   or save him from his trouble.
>
> Remember this and consider,
>   recall it to mind, you transgressors,
> remember the former things of old;
>   for I am God, and there is no other (Isa.46.6-9).

This passage, written by the Israelite prophet Isaiah, typifies the attitude taken to idols in the Bible. They, and the beliefs of the people who make them, are worth nothing when compared with the only and true God. They can't really help a man when he's in trouble. How could they, being the products of man's own invention? Only one god deserves man's worship, and that is the God who made him. This attitude is maintained right through to the New Testament. But here the bonnet of idolatry is lifted and we get to look down on the engine of these false faiths. Listen to Paul the apostle advising the early church on idolatry:

> Therefore, my beloved, shun the worship of idols. I
> speak as to sensible men ... are not those who eat the
> sacrifices partners in the altar? What do I imply then?
> That food offered to idols is anything? ... No. I imply
> that what pagans sacrifice, they offer to demons and not
> to God. I do not want you to be partners with demons.
> (1 Cor.10.14,15,18-20).

Here we are coming down to the raw truth of the matter. Idols –
or alternative religions – are not merely empty and mistaken
beliefs. That in itself would be bad enough. In fact they are
traps, recruitment agencies for the forces of the Devil. Again, I
don't mean to question the integrity of individuals involved in
them (though in many cases it would be appropriate to do that);
I merely want to point out that there are many ways of achieving
closer alignment with the Devil, even if you start out with no
conscious intention of doing so, and that religions denying the
Christian faith offer one such way.

But there is a fourth approach to the supernatural, one that is
at the same moment more direct and more deadly. The decoration is stripped away, and the enquirer knows full well what he
is letting himself in for. In fact he begins with the stated intention of *serving the Devil*. This is the most basic and rank form of
idolatry; not a vague and misinformed searching for false gods,
but a deliberate courting of evil. Ultimately, this *Satanism* is the
fulfilment of all the Devil's hopes, since in wishing to take the
place of God nothing pleases him better than to receive the free
worship that is properly reserved for the Creator.

It is significant, though, that even in Satanism, where one
would expect the believer to be best informed of the Devil's
purposes, there is almost no comprehension of who the Devil
really is. Little hint is given of the conflict between Satan and
God; the Satanic Bible pictures God as an impersonal being
with no interest in the welfare of mankind. As such, Satanism
reduces itself to a cult of self-gratification – doing whatever you
want, just because you want to – and pays no attention to wider
issues. It is fairly easy to see what is happening. The Satanist is
kept in the dark as to the real state of affairs and through his
imagined freedom is infused with the rebellious and hideously
corrupt nature of the Devil himself. Satan, after all, is self-

gratification in its purest form.

This element of deception is common to all of the approaches to the supernatural we have looked at. As far as the Devil is concerned there is a news blackout on the spiritual world. No one is allowed to know what is really going on. The whole system depends on a carefully organised propaganda campaign – discrediting Christian belief and playing on people's curiosity about the supernatural, their fears about the future, and their natural urge to better themselves. But to make an approach to the Devil's forces in even the most trivial way is fantastically dangerous, for two reasons.

The first, I hope, has been made sufficiently clear by my own story. The realm presided over by Satan is no garden of delights. You may be tempted into it by a desire for power or wealth, by curiosity, lust, or respectable and humanitarian motives. It makes no difference. Service for the Devil is slavery, as you will quickly discover if, as I did, you attempt to get out. You are there on the Devil's terms, not your own. You may cling fondly to the notion that you can bring pressure on supernatural forces by certain charms and prayers; but in reality you are as helpless as a prisoner in a labour camp. And in the end you will die a prisoner's death: without hope.

The second reason is that an approach to Satan is an act of overt rebellion against God. It is true, of course, that in a very important sense we have *all* become rebels, cut off from the one source of goodness and life. But being superstitious, wearing a lucky charm or consulting a medium are acts of special defiance. Think of it this way. We live in occupied territory; our world has been overrun by an alien and evil spiritual force. As a result some influence of evil has crept into our life and behaviour in a way that is almost beyond our control. But we don't have to co-operate with the enemy; we are free to work against him if we want to, and we are free to comply with him. The choice is ours. And to make any of the approaches to Satan described above is a definite act of compliance – collaborating with the occupying force.

This probably explains the severity of God's judgment on such practices. Here, for example, is an extract from the Law that God gave to his special people, the Israelites, in the second millennium BC. What it tells us about God's attitude is still true today.

> There shall not be found among you any one who burns his son or his daughter as an offering, and any one who practises divination, a soothsayer, or an augur, or a sorcerer, or a charmer, or a medium, or a wizard, or a necromancer. For whoever does these things is an abomination to the Lord (Deut.18.10-12).

The word 'abomination' denotes all that is in utter contradiction of the good, all that is contrary to the nature of God. Another version translates it 'detestable'. God did not want man — especially the Israelites, who were entrusted with his work — to have any dealings with the Devil. Anyone who did came in for a very severe punishment. That punishment was meted out at the hands of appointed judges, just as crime today is dealt with in the law courts. But rebellion against God is something that has consequences far beyond this present world. Those who during the course of their life align themselves with the Devil will, when the spiritual war is over, suffer the same punishment as the Devil — that of eternal separation from God. And that means not the mixture of good and bad of which our earthly lives are made up, but an existence ruled and surrounded by evil alone. It is the rejection of God's goodness taken to its logical conclusion.

But this judgment, this final reckoning, comes right at the end of history. It is the *coup de grâce* by which God is going to destroy the Devil's work on this earth and begin an age of world-wide peace. By then the spiritual war will be over. But that leaves a large part of the story untold. How is God now winning back the world Satan overran in the distant past? The answer to this question is extremely significant for us all, and it is this we are going to examine in the last chapter.

10: The Devil and you

We have seen already how the whole human race, including you and I, has rebelled against God and decided to please itself. Ironically, it is by this desire to put ourselves first that the Devil holds sway over us, and makes us secret sympathisers with his cause even when we know nothing about the war that's going on in the supernatural world. As a teenager I never understood this. It was only when I went to Watford that I came to see a connection between my own behaviour and what the Bible called 'sin'.

This sin seems to have been passed down the generations, and it emerges in the behaviour of every human being as naturally as the desire to eat. It seems so natural, in fact, that we are tempted to dismiss it as part of the human character and say, 'That's just what people are like'. Well, of course, it *is* — but it's not what people are *supposed* to be like. We grasp that point easily enough when the sins people commit are embarrassingly ugly. Nearly everyone disapproves of robbery, rape and murder, and we regard anyone who doesn't as having a warped personality.

But sin is present in many of the day-to-day actions we all take for granted. If you don't believe me, take ten minutes and do some honest thinking about your own way of life. If you're up to it you'll reach some surprising conclusions. Think about your relationship with the people around you, at home, at school, at college, at work. Do you never act hurtfully towards them? Can you be relied upon to keep your word and pay your debts? And what about that expense account — how much of it *really* goes on the business? Are you proud? Do you like people to think highly of you when you don't deserve it? And how do you look at others? Does it give you a kick to gossip about them and criticise them? Can you honestly say you don't envy someone else's salary, success or good looks? Perhaps you think yourself a cut above the average; if so, do you take advantage of another person because they 'asked for it' or because 'business life is like that'? And what will you do to win someone's sexual favours? How do you relate to the underprivileged – the old, the unemployed, the slow, the weak, the crippled? Do you try to help them, or do you make jokes about them, avoid them or try not to think about them?

These are just a few of the difficult questions we may ask ourselves. There are many more. Thinking about them you will probably come to the conclusion that you do not always do what you know you 'ought' to. That is true of me and, like me, I expect you will find it very hard to admit you're in the wrong. If you do admit it you will likely want to justify yourself. 'I know I shouldn't do that,' you'll say, 'but ... '

Now excuses can be genuine, but it's a very rare thing! Have a closer look at some of your 'buts'.

'Everyone else does it.' Yes, but does that mean *you* should do it? Suppose everyone else was putting on a stocking mask and robbing old ladies at gunpoint. Would you follow suit? Wrong is wrong, after all.

'Yes, all right. But there's surely a difference between big wrongs and small ones. Nobody minds the small ones.' Nobody? I bet you'd be the first to complain if someone did *you* down! Small wrongs have a way of looking pretty big when you're the victim. Why not stop doing them to others?

'OK, I agree. But be reasonable. I'm trying as hard as I can already.' Are you ... ?

You see, the problem with excuses is that we make them much too easily. There are a lot of nasty things inside us that we prefer to keep hidden, and excuses provide a convenient way of covering them up. Stripped of our excuses we have to admit we're pretty self-centred creatures. Some would argue that this doesn't matter: evolution has made us that way and the world is little the worse for it. But is that really true? Despite what the television tells us the world is an unhappy place for most of its inhabitants, and the rot is there in every one of us. The indifference to the welfare of others that we condemn in dictators and criminals is only an inflated version of the indifference we ourselves express. The problems of the world don't begin with the government, or the system, or 'them'; they start with you, and me. If we all obeyed the commands God gave us – to love him, and to love those around us – we would still be in paradise. But none of us do! We go through life having to deal with mistrust, suspicion, exploitation, resentment and hurt. Mankind always has. That's why the Devil has had it almost completely his own way.

Almost.

God, you see, has mounted a rescue mission, or more precisely a counter-offensive against the Devil. One minor result of this is that the Bible is split into two parts – the Old Testament and the New. The Old Testament looks forward to the rescue, and the New Testament examines its early stages. In the days of the Old Testament it became clearer and clearer that man could not fight his own battle against Satan, and many of the prophets – the special messengers of God – began to look ahead to a time when God would send someone – the Messiah – to save the human race. There are numerous prophecies about the place where he would be born, what sort of person he would be, and what he was going to do. One of these prophecies was written by Isaiah; he imagines these words spoken by the coming Messiah:

> The Spirit of the Lord God is upon me,
>   because the Lord has anointed me
> to bring good tidings to the afflicted;
>   he has sent me to bind up the brokenhearted,
> to proclaim liberty to the captives,
>   and the opening of the prison to those who are bound;
> to proclaim the year of the Lord's favour,
>   and the day of vengeance of our God (Isa.61.1,2).

The coming Messiah, of course, was Jesus. In fact Jesus announced his arrival as God's Son by reading these very words from the Old Testament. Jesus fulfilled on every count the predictions that the prophets had made about him. In particular he was descended from the great Israelite king called David, whose rule was looked back on as a golden age by the Jews. But Jesus was far more than a very good man: he was God in human form. This is a mystery that a hundred books would not suffice to explain, so I won't attempt to. It is best summed up by saying that Jesus was 100 per cent man and 100 per cent God. In the Gospels the titles 'Son of Man' and 'Son of God' are both used to describe him. That means that it is true to say of Jesus that he was the most perfect man (in fact the *only* perfect man) who ever lived, and at the same time that he was the one Creator-God, stripping himself of his rightful glory, and stepping in an ordinary, weak human body, into the world that he had made.

He was born in about 4 BC in Bethlehem, a small town 6 miles south of Israel's capital city, Jerusalem. It was a difficult time. Israel was ruled over by an ageing and neurotic king, Herod the Great, who was himself a puppet of Rome. Rumours that the Messiah had been born near Jerusalem made him fearful that he was about to be overthrown, and he ordered, insanely, that all the young male children in Bethlehem should be killed. Jesus' family escaped by the skin of their teeth, having been warned of Herod's intentions by a dream. They moved to Egypt until Herod died, then returned not to Bethlehem but to another town about seventy miles north, called Nazareth.

Jesus grew up in a settled and peaceful home, and presumably learned his father's trade as a carpenter. One of the few surviving details from this period of his life indicates that even as a child he was extraordinarily wise. But little is said about him in the Gospels until he reached maturity, which in those times was deemed to begin at the age of thirty. It was then that he left his home to tour the country as a preacher, and his real work as God's Son got under way.

Right at the start of this period came the confrontation with the Devil that Mr Hartley taught me about. For Jesus these forty days spent without food in the desert were an important test. If he'd broken then, his whole work on earth would have been useless. Naturally the Devil, suspicious but uncertain of Jesus' intentions, did his utmost to break him. The method he used was temptation – the temptation for Jesus to abandon his difficult mission and settle for simple political glory. The last of the three temptations is especially significant:

> Again, the devil took him to a very high mountain, and showed him all the kingdoms of the world and the glory of

them; and he said to him, 'All these I will give you, if you will fall down and worship me' (Matt.4.8,9).

Notice first of all that the Devil was in a position to *give* these kingdoms. He was the undisputed ruler of the supernatural world on earth, and had he chosen he could have intervened in historical events – the course of the material world – and installed Jesus as king over the Israelites, and even over the mighty Roman Empire. But notice also the price he was asking! He wanted Jesus, the Son of God, to bow down and worship him; he required the creator of the universe to pay homage to his creation. It was for that ambition that he'd been thrown out of heaven, and here he was trying to achieve it again. Jesus gave him pretty short shrift: 'You shall worship the Lord your God, and him only shall you serve' (Matt.4.10).

That was the decisive moment. Jesus, weakened to the point of exhaustion by his ordeal in the desert, refused to give way. He asserted his authority over the Devil, and the Devil was forced to back down. A bridgehead had been established. Jesus was able to go on to his work of preaching the gospel – the good news that mankind was now to be set free – without further hindrance.

The next three years are recorded in some detail in all four Gospels. Jesus collected around him a small band of followers, men who were later to write much of the New Testament, and set about instructing them. The main thrust of his teaching concerned the 'kingdom of God' – the establishment of God's rule on the earth that began with Jesus himself and that would in the end overthrow all the powers of darkness and restore mankind to his former state. Words were backed up with action. Everywhere he went he performed healings as a sign of what God was doing to the world. The blind, the deaf, the crippled, the insane were all made well. He even called the dead back to life – in one case a man who had been rotting for four days. As a result he brought out the population in droves to listen to him – and incurred the stern disapproval of the official religious authorities. As time went on, and Jesus became progressively more popular, the tension grew. He lived in an occupied country, and many of the more radical Jews were urging him to declare a revolution and free Israel from the domination of Rome. This caused the Jewish leaders (who were very comfortable under

Roman rule) considerable anxiety. True enough, Jesus hadn't actually *said* he was going to start a revolt, but what did he mean to do? And if a revolt started among his followers, would he be able to restrain it even if he wanted to?

As the country buzzed with speculation about this incredible prophet the time came to celebrate the most important Jewish festival of the year, the Feast of the Passover. In this the Jews remembered their miraculous escape from slavery to the Egyptians about a thousand years before. Was history going to repeat itself? People gathered at Jerusalem, awaiting the arrival of Jesus. The Jewish king (another Herod) was there, as well as Pontius Pilate, the Roman procurator, who had brought with him a collection of garrisons to still any signs of unrest. The stage seemed set for some kind of showdown.

Jesus entered the city one week before the Passover. He was received by a large and cheering crowd, through which he made his way towards the temple. Here he forcibly removed all the marketeers who made a dubious living by changing money and selling animals for sacrifice. The temple, he said, was God's house and a place of prayer, not a den of robbers. This posed a direct challenge to the high priest, who for years had allowed trading in the temple. In fact by doing it Jesus was for the first time publicly claiming the authority of the Messiah.

To the religious authorities this claim was nothing short of blasphemous, and they renewed their efforts to have him put away. But Jesus' popularity worked against them; to have him arrested in public would be the quickest way to start a riot, and that would upset their precarious favour with Rome. Instead, they hung fire and awaited an opportunity to trap him.

The week wore on. Jesus went every day to the temple court and spoke before the amassed pilgrims and inhabitants of the city. He had them spellbound; no ploy used by the religious leaders could catch him out; when they tried to back him into tight corners on the matter of the Roman occupation (in the hope of forcing a treasonable remark) he deftly turned the question to face them with their own hypocrisy. His criticism of the existing religious system was devastating. He even went so far as to predict that its corruption and unbelief would result in the destruction of Jerusalem and the scattering of the Jewish race — an event that occurred some forty years later when the

Romans besieged and razed the city. All this the authorities had to take sitting down; they dared not risk the anger of the crowds. It looked as if Jesus was going to leave the city unscathed.

But then things started to go wrong. As the Passover approached one of the closest followers of Jesus, a man called Judas Iscariot, became disillusioned with the line Jesus was taking, and decided to betray him to the authorities. Why he took this decision is unclear; he seemed to feel that Jesus was not making sufficient efforts to aid the poor, though his sincerity on this is open to question since, the Gospels tell us, he was in charge of the group purse and often stole from it. At any rate it was in the confusion of Judas' mind that Satan found his opportunity. According to the Gospel of Luke, he 'entered into Judas called Iscariot' (Luke 22.37), and Judas went to the chief priests, who offered him thirty silver pieces to tell them when Jesus could be found alone and unprotected.

The chance was not long in coming. On the night of the Passover Jesus ate a meal with his closest followers, then retired with them to the garden of Gethsemane to pray. Suddenly Judas appeared at the head of an armed mob. He identified Jesus by kissing him – an ironic gesture of goodwill – upon which the mob seized their victim and took him away to the house of the high priest, Caiaphas. Here an assembly of religious leaders swiftly condemned him to death. But their sentence could not be carried out without the approval of Rome, so when dawn broke they marched on the praetorium. Pontius Pilate was unwilling to settle the dispute and as soon as he heard that Jesus was from Galilee he sent him to Herod, who was officially responsible for that part of the Jewish territories. Herod, however, merely sent Jesus back, and Pilate was forced to tackle the case himself. He seems to have found Jesus innocent, and as a compromise proposed to flog him and let him go. But a sizeable crowd had now gathered, thick with supporters of the high priest, and a cry went up that Jesus had declared himself a king, and was therefore an enemy of Rome. Had there been a shred of truth in this, Pilate could have given in to them with a clear conscience. Almost certainly he saw through their deception; but his own standing with Rome was far from secure, and rather than risk being recalled himself he allowed Jesus – a man he confessed to be innocent of all charges – to die the death of a common criminal.

The method was crucifixion. Jesus was made to carry his own cross out of the city to a hill called Golgotha. There he was stripped and nailed by the hands and feet to the rough post and crossbeam that was the standard means of execution for all offenders who were not citizens of Rome. He hung on this Roman gibbet, derided by his enemies, until about three o'clock in the afternoon when he died. There was no doubt that he died. To make sure, one of the Roman soldiers on guard duty shoved a spear into his side, and the blood that flowed out was separated. Later that day some of his followers came to take the body down, wrapped it in a winding sheet, and laid it in a tomb, rolling a heavy stone against the entrance. The Son of God had been killed.

That is why the Guide tried to tell me that Jesus was just a dead body, that the Devil had defeated him. Certainly the moment of Christ's death must have seemed to the Devil a moment of supreme victory. But it was short-lived. And if he had paid more attention to events preceding the Crucifixion he might have known why.

You see, death didn't come as a surprise to Jesus. For months before his death he had been telling his followers he was going to be betrayed and handed over to the Romans and crucified. It was his deliberate purpose in going up to Jerusalem. But of course no one believed him; they all thought his words had some mystical significance and that in fact Jesus was going to take over from the Romans and found his kingdom in an immediate, political sense. Even when on the night of the Passover Jesus identified Judas as his betrayer and told him to go out and do what he had to do, the other followers thought Judas was being sent out to get some more food. For Jesus to give himself up to death when such tremendous opportunities lay open before him was just plain stupid, and they wouldn't accept it.

The execution of Jesus was a move in the spiritual war that came as a complete shock, and it remains one of the central paradoxes of Christianity. God chose defeat as a means to victory; he allowed his Son Jesus Christ to be killed in the battle because that was the one move that would guarantee complete success. This is turning any sane theory of war on its head. No military strategist, still less the Devil, would expect his enemy to

146

fall, helpless, at his feet as a means to winning the war. In human terms such a method would be mere suicide. But God's mind works on a level far above that of the human. As Paul the apostle wrote to the Church of Corinth a few years later, 'None of the rulers of this age understood this; for if they had, they would not have crucified the Lord of glory' (1 Cor.2.8). The phrase 'rulers of this age' might refer equally well to the Roman and Jewish authorities or to the Devil who, as we know, is the *real* ruler behind earthly power. Certainly the Devil would not have crucified Jesus if he had known that this very triumph would be his undoing.

But in what way was Jesus' death a success? How could he achieve anything simply by dying? The answer is that he died in our place. We have said already that the whole human race has rebelled and stands under the judgment of God. Every one of us is guilty. But Jesus' death cleared us of that guilt. It may help you to understand this if you picture yourself in an ordinary court of law, and facing prosecution.

Imagine that you have been brought to trial, and are standing in the dock. The court-room is silent and rather gloomy. The prosecution has rested his case and the jury has passed the unanimous verdict that you are guilty. There is no doubt about it; you have nothing to gain by an appeal. All that remains is for the judge to give his sentence. The old man clears his throat and addressing you by name catalogues the offences you are guilty of. It goes on for a very long time. When he finishes all the lawyers sit with eyes downcast, their white wigs as still as the thick, wooden rail of the dock. At last the judge gets round to summing up.

'You have heard the charges brought against you. No one in this room doubts that you are guilty of every single one of them. I am sorry that you did not see fit to use your freedom more wisely. As it is, I find it my unpleasant but unavoidable duty ... ' (he leans forward, clasping his hands together in front of him) ' ... to sentence you to death.'

You find yourself examining in great detail the knotty grain of the wood beneath your fingers. A slim ray of sunshine falling on the rail raises it from a dull brown to amber. Suddenly that seems very important to you. The rest of the court-room is motionless and silent. You wonder if you ought to be saying something. And then you feel your arms grasped firmly from behind by the policemen who brought you.

At that moment the judge stands up. 'Wait!' he calls. You look up and see him removing his wig, his gown and his tie. The change is astounding. All of a sudden he looks just like you – an ordinary human being. You watch him step down from the dais and cross the court-room to join you in the dock. He places his hand on those of the policemen to signify that they should leave. They do so. Now you are confused, wondering if this is normal procedure, and what it all means. He is looking you straight in the eye. 'I'm giving you a second chance,' he says. 'Your crimes deserve the death penalty, and justice demands that the penalty be paid. However, if you want, I will take your place and go to the gallows myself. I make the offer freely. If you accept, you will leave this court a free man. The choice is yours.'

What would you do? Or rather, what *will* you do, because what I have tried to picture in this scene is exactly what Jesus has done for you, and for me, by his death on the cross. If we accept his offer, the penalty for our rebellion, our sins, falls upon him: he dies in our place. In that case, all that the Devil has sought to accomplish in your life is undone. You live from that moment on as a free man or woman. The writer of one book in the New Testament explains it this way:

> ... he himself likewise partook of the same nature, that
> through death he might destroy him who has the power
> of death, that is, the devil, and deliver all those who
> through fear of death were subject to lifelong bondage
> (Heb.2.14,15).

But that isn't all. The judge in my story, once he had died, would have stayed dead. Not so Jesus. When, three days after the Crucifixion, some women came to treat the body of Jesus with spices, they found the great stone at the tomb entrance rolled aside, and the winding sheet lying exactly where it had been placed – with nothing inside it. Jesus had gone.

His absence from the tomb, of course, is no proof that he had come back to life. Scholars who have examined the problem on the assumption that resurrection is impossible – in other words, who think that the idea of rising from the dead is simply ridiculous — have come up with some ingenious explanations for the empty tomb. Some suggest that Jesus wasn't really dead, after all, and escaped from the tomb when he recovered from a swoon; others consider it more likely that someone else stole the body. Several writers have weighed up the evidence for these theories at more length than I can do here, but we must acknowledge that none of them is in factual terms very likely. A half-dead man would hardly have sufficient strength to push a boulder from the mouth of a tomb; and who, in the end, would have anything to gain by stealing the corpse? His followers, perhaps. But something pretty queer would have to be going on in their minds if, after faking the Resurrection, they went to the ends of the known world preaching about it and refused to deny their belief even on pain of death.

But there is quite another area of evidence that we have to take into account here. Not only did Jesus disappear from the tomb: he also appeared, alive and well, to a large number of his followers. He talked to them, ate with them, and invited them to touch his resurrected body. There is something hearteningly authentic about one follower of Jesus, called Thomas, who refused to believe the reports about Jesus' resurrection until he had placed his own finger in the marks made by the nails. When, eight days later, he was given the opportunity, he refused!

If Jesus had been seen only once by just a few of his followers the Resurrection could be dismissed as a product of hallucination. But read this extract from Paul's first letter to the Corinthians:

> For I delivered to you as of first importance what I also
> received, that Christ died for our sins in accordance
> with the scriptures, that he was buried, that he was
> raised on the third day in accordance with the
> scriptures, and that he appeared to Cephas, then to the
> twelve. Then he appeared to more than five hundred
> brethren at one time, most of whom are still alive,
> though some have fallen asleep. Then he appeared to
> James, then to all the apostles. Last of all, as to one
> untimely born, he appeared also to me (1 Cor.15.3-8).

Paul wrote this letter not more than twenty-five years after

Christ's death. Had you been a member of the Corinthian Church you could have visited some of the 500 or so 'brethren', or followers of Jesus, to substantiate Paul's claim. Many of them would have seen Jesus after his death, talked to him and eaten with him, on more than one occasion. Some would have seen him return to his Father in heaven. They were, at least, all sufficiently convinced of the Resurrection to go round the world convincing others and even to suffer death for their beliefs. Were they really imagining it all? Were they really founding a religion that they knew for a fact to be completely false?

Try as we might, it is extremely difficult to explain the evidence away. Could it be that Jesus really *did* rise from the dead? In a self-assured and materialistic age like ours people are apt to reply on instinct that resurrection is impossible. It seems to run counter to science, and our obstinate refusal to believe anything that cannot be 'proved'. And yet science doesn't pretend to tell us anything about things that are not capable of proof; and we must accept that the world contains many things that cannot be proved in the scientific sense. Science won't tell you whether you love someone, or whether Julius Caesar invaded Britain. Those kinds of truth come across to us in completely different ways. The Roman invasion is an *historical* truth; like Christ's resurrection we know about it because someone who was around at the time took the trouble to record the event. Whether we believe it or not depends on the degree of our faith in the source. We might ask ourselves whether the historian in question actually witnessed the events himself, or picked them up from other people. If the latter, were *his* sources reliable? On this count, the Resurrection comes out a lot better than many things we consider to be established history.

On the other hand, when we say to a person, 'I love you', we are communicating a *personal* truth. Our love doesn't require proof, because we demonstrate it through our attitudes and actions. You would be most put out if, bouquet in hand, you declared your love for your valentine, only to be presented with a notepad and pocket calculator and a demand to 'prove it'! Even if you tried you couldn't do it. Love cannot be proved by science.

Now both these sorts of truth are relevant to Christianity. We have already mentioned the historical evidence for the Resurrection. We have not 'proved' that it occurred, but we have provided the sort of evidence that, in a court of law, might be considered adequate to condemn, or acquit, a criminal. We have, if you like, cross-examined the witnesses. But it doesn't stop there. The Resurrection isn't simply a remarkable fact to be filed away in the *Guinness Book of Records*. It has earth-shattering consequences. It is as important to the human race as news about D-Day was to occupied France, or the British Task Force was to the besieged islanders of the Falklands. It is the hope of freedom, the beginning of a revolutionary new offensive in the spiritual war. No one who lives on the Falklands took the news about the Task Force as a neutral fact. Everybody committed themselves wholeheartedly to supporting the invasion.

In the same way, Christ's resurrection demands from us a *personal* response. We either support what God is doing in the world, or we remain indifferent and so hinder it. But there is more to it even than this, because in the spiritual war to commit yourself to God is to begin a personal relationship with him. Incredibly, we tiny individuals are privileged to know the Creator. We are, to use an analogy, introduced to our commander-in-chief and expected to keep in close liaison with him. And he provides us with all the support we need to fight effectively.

What does this mean in practice? The answer is provided once again by Paul, writing this time to the Church at Rome, on the subject of Christ's death and resurrection:

> Do you not know that all of us who have been baptized into Christ Jesus were baptized into his death? We were buried therefore with him by baptism into death, so that as Christ was raised from the dead by the glory of the Father, we too might walk in newness of life (Rom.6.3,4).

His reasoning is complex. What he is saying is that when a person becomes a Christian and is baptised – that is, washed clean in a symbolic way of his rebellion against God – he is really undergoing a kind of death. As far as his old way of life is concerned he is a dead man, he is finished. That part of his nature is effectively buried with Christ. But even as Christ was raised up again, so the Christian receives a completely new life, an inner life to which physical death is not an ending but merely a door to a closer presence with God. He has, spiritually, been born again.

In one way this re-birth is a total transformation, as total as that of a caterpillar into a butterfly. In another way it is the beginning of a long, hard road. The Christian is not simply a new man or a new woman; he, or she, is a new recruit to God's commando force. When we take the momentous step of becoming Christians we accept a new lifestyle. We join the counter-offensive that Jesus began with his strange victory on the cross.

In the past some Christians have taken the idea of warfare quite literally. They often thought that the best way they could contribute to Christ's work was to go off to the Crusades and drive the 'pagans' out of God's holy city, Jerusalem. Unfortunately this more often resulted in a bloodbath than in any real progress in the supernatural war. Paul tells us very clearly in his letter to the Church at Ephesus that

> we are not contending against flesh and blood, but
> against the principalities, against the powers, against
> the world rulers of this present darkness, against the
> spiritual hosts of wickedness in the heavenly places
> (Eph.6.12).

In this sort of warfare swords and guns are useless. We need a very different sort of weaponry, one in which the best defences are moral goodness and a firm faith in God. These are the only things that will keep out the sort of bullets the Devil is likely to fire at us. And the battle itself is fought very largely on a supernatural plane. There are four main areas of conflict: prayer, lifestyle, evangelism and deliverance.

Prayer is the equivalent of the two-way radio. It is what keeps the Christian in contact with base. Through it he can tell God about the difficulties he is facing, ask for help, and say thanks for the support he's getting. It is a source of strength and guidance, especially when a group of Christians crowd round the 'radio' together. But more than this, prayer, consistently applied, can influence the course of events. Christians can pray for healing, for employment, for their nation, for the relief of world poverty and the averting of natural disasters. It's tough and necessary work. Anyone who's tried it will know how hard prayer can be. The Devil uses all his resources to stop it happening. So it needs application. Some of the most famous Christians, like Augustine, Luther and Wesley, spent hours on their knees. Prayer is definitely a form of battle.

So too is lifestyle. The Christian is a brand-new person, living with a mind and body used to the old regime. He may have been born again, but the old habits still dog him. He finds himself still strongly tempted to all the rebellious activities we looked at earlier in this chapter. He is used to them, though they are no longer part of his true self. Paul talked about every Christian as having an 'old nature' and a 'new nature'; they are like sets of clothes: the one, an old set that no longer fits him, he has to take off; the other, a new, fresh set suited to his new status, he has consciously to put on. Here again, the Devil has an interest in resisting the change. Under his direction old habits die very hard indeed. And while we can't blame our failures on Satan, it is undoubtedly true that he places temptation in our way. By adopting a new lifestyle we use the same power that belonged to Jesus when he met the Devil in the wilderness and fight to overcome our adversary in the same way.

As for evangelism, that means nothing more than 'telling the good news'. Christians are messengers sent to show that Christ is good news for the human race. Paul, in a letter to the Corinthian Church, describes them as ambassadors. They carry out a sort of diplomatic peace mission to their friends and neighbours, telling them that Jesus is putting this twisted world to rights: bringing forgiveness for wrong; healing for broken relationships; freedom for those held captive by sadness and depression; new life for the tired and lonely. In short, telling them that Jesus is undoing the Devil's work. This, of course, is good news for everyone but the Devil, and he employs every means at his disposal to make sure that no one else hears it. We may be quite right to regard atheism and political repression as a natural consequence of human sin, but it is certain from the biblical standpoint that they are fostered by the 'spiritual hosts of wickedness'. The Devil is a staunch supporter of anything that will prevent the Christian from speaking out, or breed cynicism in his hearers.

But the Devil's control over some human lives is far more

direct than that. If a person strays too far into the more blatantly anti-Christian practices, such as spiritism, Satanism or witch-craft, he may become so strongly aligned with the rebellious forces that they are able to infiltrate his mind and body. The biblical word for this state is best translated 'demonisation', or 'affliction by demons', although older versions of the Bible use the phrase 'possessed of evil spirits'. It doesn't usually mean that the victim becomes a helpless machine, unable to control his own actions. Sometimes a demonised person will just feel un-easy, as if another person is in the room with him when he's alone. In most cases, like my own, demonisation is something between the two, a partial invasion by evil personalities who exercise a degree of control over their host but do not completely take him over. These personalities are not dead people; they are minions of the Devil, lesser angels who joined in his rebellion and are referred to in the New Testament as demons.

Demonisation is not a psychiatric disorder, though it is frequently mistaken for one. No amount of electroconvulsive therapy, anti-depressants, hypnosis or psychoanalysis will cure it, any more than these things will remove a fishbone caught in the throat. The only way to cure the demoniac is to get rid of the demons. This treatment is popularly known as exorcism, but a far better word for it is deliverance. Why? Because removing demons is not a clinical operation that depends on the technique and skill of the practitioner: it is a matter of spiritual authority. There is no prayer, formula, geometrical figure, symbol, incense or incantation that will make a demon budge one inch. You might as well do conjuring tricks as a means of entry into the Kremlin. The only way to remove a demon is to stand in the power and authority of the one by whom the Devil's forces have already been decisively defeated – Jesus. On that night in Watford Mr Williams didn't recite a magic formula; nor did he pray for healing or for a vague and general victory over Satan, as the other Christians had done. He addressed the demons directly, as a warrior of Christ: 'I command every evil spirit in this man to come out now, *in the name of Jesus.*' He wasn't using the name superstitiously; he spoke with all the powers of heaven assembled at his back. He was officially telling the demons to leave, because the place they occupied didn't belong to them any more.

There are two very important things to pick up here. First, the person who carries out the ministry of deliverance has to be a Christian. Not just a believer in God; not just a person with a lot of faith; not just an exorcist. Only a Christian has the authority that the Devil is forced to respect. And not all Christians should take on a deliverance lightly, because deliverance is a very direct and brutal assault on Satan, which will invite fierce resistance. The Christian should be a mature and devoted servant of God. The second thing has to do with the demoniac. Remember that there is no neutral ground in the spiritual war; to be an 'ordinary' person, or an agnostic, is in fact to inhabit the outer fringes of the Devil's realm. He may not visit the fringes very often, but they still belong to him! It follows that a person who is delivered cannot return to his former, non-religious life. He has been liberated, and if he is not to fall back under the power of his captors he must join the liberators. He must, in short, become a Christian. That is why popular exorcism of the sort that is written about in paperback novels is completely useless. To be exorcised in this way is to exchange one sort of devilry for another. The person treated in this way is merely changing concentration camps.

That's not to say that becoming a Christian is easy, whether you come to Jesus from spiritism or simply apathy. To the Devil it's a step in the wrong direction, and he will do his utmost to discourage and frighten you. Most Christians would probably agree that life has become harder, not easier, since they were converted. At the same time, this new life that Jesus gives his followers is amazingly rich and fulfilling. And there is no skirmish with the Devil, in deliverance or temptation, that they do not have the power to win.

On the day I went chasing through London in search of Jesus this advice given to Christians by the apostle James would have seemed incredible to me: 'Resist the devil and he will flee from you' (Js.4.7). And yet that was exactly what the Devil had to do before Jesus in the wilderness, and it's what he has to do before Christians today. The fact is that with Jesus we are on the winning side. The time will come when the rebellious forces who long ago were thrown down from heaven are rounded up, and the evils of the world subjected to judgment. Until then, if you are a Christian, you are engaged in a war, rescuing fellow

155

men and women from the rebels. It may be that God puts you, as he did me, in that particular sort of work where it is necessary to confront and cast out evil spirits. But that is only one part of the battlefield, and there are many more.

And if you are not a Christian? In that case I hope this book has helped to make you aware of the dimensions of the spiritual conflict that goes on unseen within this world. I must say that as a teenager, listening to dear old Mr Hartley, I never got a very clear idea of who the Devil was. Somehow he didn't seem very important. And yet to consider the Devil is to consider questions of cosmic importance, not least the nature and origin of the evil that is so widespread in our world. The human race has become a battleground over which the forces of good and evil are locked in mortal combat. In one sense, then, we are the booty that goes to the winner and have little say in the overall course of events; yet in another we ourselves decide the outcome. Each of us is a small part of the field, and on our our territory that decision is very largely ours. This being the case, as far as you as an individual are concerned, the problem resolves itself into very simple terms: the Devil wants your soul.

Are you going to give it to him?